The Empaths
Guidebook to Consciousness and Awareness

Jamie Bates

www.jamie-bates.com

Copyright © 2019 Jamie Bates. www.jamie-bates.com
Cover art and book layout by Andrea Dombecki

The information provided in this book are the personal views of Jamie Bates from New You Reality LLC. These views are for informational purposes only. If at any point the views within this information do not work for you please just leave it and move on. Any and all the information contained within this site is meant to give you more space of you. It is not a substitution for any type of treatment. It is not a substitute for the advice of your doctor, lawyer, accountant, or any of your advisors, public or private. Thank you.

Contents

Dedications	6
Forward	7
Introduction	8
Chapter 1: Stories to expand your reality	9
What's going on in this reality	9
Why are you here and why should you stay	11
How much of you is present in this reality	18
Getting clear about who you are	21
Why being an empath is such a gift	26
Chapter 2: Tools you can use	29
Being present with your body	29
Stop protecting start expanding	32
Stay expanded and receive everything	34
What if you could just remove stuff?	38
Clearing out your garden	43
Your body is a receiving organ	56
Asking questions to actualize anything	65
Feeling your truth	68
Learning to ask questions for heavy and light	72

Pulling and Receiving	78
Chapter 3: Healing your body and being	83
Expansion of who you be	83
Stop resisting what you know	85
What do I know about me?	91
Stop caring what other people choose	94
Clearing your space of upset with someone else	96
Removing connection points to you	100
Letting you off the hook	104
Get out of conclusion	108
Just because you hear it in your head	111
Everything has a reason	115
Projections and Expectations	118
When expectations create separations	122
Chapter 4: Untangling the lies of this reality	125
Lies or information that is not true	125
Forgiveness	127
Trust	128
There is something wrong with you	130
You have to figure everything out	132

You have to have a reason to say no	135
Emotional upset is normal	136
Love is the answer	141
Life is a struggle	142
Perpetrating the wrongness	143
Autoresponders of wrongness	146
Chapter 5: Get clear about what you want to create	148
Choice creates	148
Get clear about what you want to create	154
Stop letting others affect your life	161
Permission to choose	163
Get out of conclusion	165
Don't make money wrong	166
Getting out of money upset	168
Conscious clearings for money to show up	169
Allowing the universe to gift you	173
What to choose now?	175
About the Author	177

Dedications

To the person who feels abandoned, alone and hopeless.
To the person who is drowning in guilt, pain and overwhelm.
To the person who is ready to dive into real change.
This book is for you.

To my wonderful husband, thank you for working so hard so I can do something different. The life we are building is my absolute favorite. I love that I get to spend my life with someone who grows and learns with me. So much gratitude for you. I appreciate you more than words can say.

To my three beautiful daughters, thank you for choosing me to be your mommy. Thank you for teaching me so much about life, gratitude and contribution. I am so grateful for each of you.

To my family, thank you for standing by me and helping me to find my path. So grateful for you all.

And my clients and my friends, thank you for allowing me to grow and facilitate you all. Your contributions have created so much in my life. So grateful for you.

Forward

Your soul is tired. I see you. I feel you.

I know first hand the pain and upset you have experienced in this reality.
I know the yearning for something greater.
I know the pain of feeling emotional upset everywhere you look.

You are overwhelmed and overprocessed.
I understand first hand how hard it can be when you long for change.

You don't want to feel like a crazy person.
You don't want to respond in the way you respond. You are tired of feeling the pain of everyone around you.
You are just plain sick and tired of living the same life over and over.
You are tired of feeling guilty, sad and depressed.
Your soul is tired. I see you. I feel you.

An empath is defined as a person with the paranormal ability to apprehend the mental or emotional state of another individual.

As an empath you are aware. You deeply feel everything. The only "problem" with that is no one has taught you how to feel everything.

No one has shown you how to have ease with it.
No one has taught you how to process through emotion.
No one has invited you into the gift of being aware really is.
Until today. This is your invitation.
This book is your guide to a new life.

Introduction

This book is a journey. A journey to awaken your soul, empower your being and allow the truth of who you are to emerge. This book is a healing journey capable of taking you through the depths of emotional upset into the space of feeling healed and in control of your life.

Within these pages are the stories and tools I have used to help heal those I come into contact with that create ripples of change and transformation. This is the truth as I know it to be.

My goal for this book is to share how easy it can be to create massive waves of change in your life. I also desire for you to feel supported on your journey to consciousness and awareness. My intention is to untangle all the information you have misidentified. Really exposing the truth of your journey. When you can see what you have experienced from a different angle it allows emotional upsets and struggles to fade away. Releasing these paradigms reveal a stronger, more relaxed version of you to emerge.

It's time for you to see how very amazing, capable and strong you really are. I want you to know that you are not bad and wrong. There is nothing wrong with you. These words are my contribution to help you go beyond limitations, stand in your knowing and expand your consciousness.

As we go through the following chapters allow your being to relax into the paradigms of what is true for you. If any of the information in these chapters does not resonate with you, that's ok, skip it and go to what does. This is also an important lesson, take what works for you in life and leave what doesn't.

Chapter 1
Stories to expand your reality

"What is going on in this reality? Has everyone gone mad?"

You may be asking yourself these questions.
We are in a very powerful time of transformation.
An awakening of who we are and why we are here.

In December of 2012, we had a very powerful pole shift, the earth's axis shifted six degrees. This ended a chapter in the earth's history. The transformation began in the core, the third-dimensional frequencies stopped, and the earth started receiving higher level frequencies. This transformation has been a subtle shift with slow frequency downloads. It is said to not be done until December of 2021, in which time the Earth will be fully fifth dimensional.

This nine-year cycle is creating the earth at a new energy, a new space, and a new consciousness.

What does this mean for each of us individually? It means we are evolving as the planet is. This is a slow process for us as well. Our bodies shift slowly with the earth. As the earth evolves so do we. If this process happened overnight, the effects would have been so powerful it would have killed us all. As we would not have been able to assimilate these energies that fast. This process is allowing each of us a chance to evolve and awaken to a new energy, new space and a new consciousness.

Although I do not have full awareness of where this journey is taking us, I am aware that much of the reality as we know it, will no longer exist. The information I have received is that as we transcend into higher levels, fifth dimension and up, many things we currently experience, such as abuse, murder, and so on will no longer exist. Our lives as we know them will move to empowerment and enlightenment, coming into the oneness paradigm. Much of the upset will fade away, and we will learn to embrace peace, ease and the joy of embodiment.

This story is here to assist you to step into being the creator of your own reality. You will be reclaiming and owning who you are, what you came here for, and harnessing the power to create a reality that works for you. I am honored you are here with me, diving into many different concepts. This journey will assist you in unlocking the true space of who you be, as the infinite being you be.

Why are you here and why should you stay?

Have you ever questioned, why you are here and why should you stay? Have you ever felt like you just don't belong in this reality? Have you looked around at what other people are creating and questioned why it seems so easy for them yet so hard for you? Why are you here? And why in the world are you staying?

This universe is one of many.

I like to think of all the universes together as one huge pie. This universe would be a very small piece of this huge pie. If you can read along in the story and try to perceive what is light and true for you. If the concept of asking questions and perceiving energy is new to you, you may have a difficulty with the next few sections. Just read along and see if the conclusion feels true for you.

I like to play in the concept that all the universes together are one huge pie. Every universe out there including this universe. This universe is one very small piece of this very large pie.

If you can imagine this pie, what section of the pie would you as a being be from?

Allow yourself to perceive this information in your body, light is always true for you, heavy is always false.

Read aloud,
"Truth, am I from the whole pie? A piece of the pie? Or this section of the universe piece of pie?"

Pause and ask that again.
"Truth, am I from the whole pie? A piece of the pie? Or this section of the universe piece of pie?"

Take a deep breath and allow yourself to perceive what feels light in your body. You may not be able to perceive yet what is light and true for you and that's okay. Just take a deep breathe and keep going. If you are reading this book, you are more than likely from the whole pie.

You are from all the universes.

Feel that for a moment.

You are from more than just this universe.

Does that make you feel lighter or heavier? Take a deep breath and really allow that thought to sink into your body.

You are from all universes.

Now let's look at this whole pie, all the universes.

How many universes would you be looking at?

Perceive this in your body and ask,
"How many universes am I from? More than 5,000 universes? Or less than 5,000 universes?"

Take a deep breath and ask again.

"How many universes am I from? More than 5,000 universes? Or less than 5,000?"

Take a deep breath and really feel that.

Could it be possible you are a being from more than 5,000 universes?

Can you imagine?

Feel that for a moment. Can you perceive how light and true that is for you?

You are being from more than 5,000 universes. How amazing does that feel? Pretty expansive right?

Continuing on that thought, if you can sit for a moment with the idea that there may be different types of beings on this planet, it might explain why you feel so different.

There are infinite beings like you and I, from the whole pie, we are the empathic people.

Then there are piece of pie beings, beings from more than just this universe.

And then there are earth beings, beings from only this piece of pie.

I will explain each type of being, but it's important to know that no type of being is better than the other. They are just different types of beings. Its like farm animals, there are pigs, horses, and cows. They exist together, they have different characteristics, but one is not greater than the other. The main difference between these beings is the amount of information that each being can receive.

The whole pie beings, these are the empaths. Empathic people receive information from everyone and everything. You are an empathic person.

You are highly overstimulated because you receive information multi dimensionally, from all aspects of all universes.

You are literally receiving information from everyone and everything all the time. This is why it can be so cumbersome to be around large groups of people or out in public in general. You are continuously stimulated with information that you have not been taught how to deal with properly. On the pages of this book, I will teach you a new way to be with who you are that will create ease with being empathic.

There are beings from some universes. These beings are different in that they only receive information from some sources, not all sources as we do. Not to categorize them as all bad, because they surely are not, but one example I feel we can all relate to is someone who runs a company that poisons our food. The beings that run this company are definitely not like us and they are definitely not earth beings. These beings are from some universes and cannot receive certain frequencies. It's almost as though they cannot identify with what their actions are creating. They have no remorse for what they are choosing because they cannot receive the frequency they are creating. They literally have no awareness. Even though the proof is evident. If you can't receive it, you cannot believe it.

Then there are earth beings. Earth beings can only perceive information from this dimension and this universe. This universe seems to be easy for them. They do not struggle with overwhelming emotion like you do. Life seems easier for them because they are having a one-dimensional experience here. They master this experience easier as it is their home mission.

You, however, are different, often causing over processing and overwhelm. As we expand on these concepts further in this story, you will continue to expand creating a greater ability to process information, creating greater ease within your body and your being.

Now you're probably thinking okay, if I am a being from more than 5,000 universes what in the world am I doing showing up all small and limited in this universe?

Here's what I know:
- This universe is a frequency based light spectrum universe.
- There is no other universe exactly like this one.
- You are here because you wanted to be here.
- You are in this world, this universe right this minute because you choose to be.
- You came here just like I did, to become a master of the concepts in this universe.
- You made agreements, commitments, and oaths to come to this frequency based light realm to learn to master the different frequencies this planet has to offer.
- You also agreed that when it was time you would play a part in helping this planet evolve and wake up to the free and sovereign beings that you truly be.

What you have been living is a process of experiences. You have been having multidimensional light based experiences. Everything this planet has to offer is an experience. Every struggle, every upset, every moment of joy, have all been a part of the experience of this reality.

As a being from more than 5,000 universes, there is no possible way you could have came here at the space that you truly be and exist in this reality. Prior to being embodied, you chose different beings and different ways that you would lock up and limit yourself. You came to play in this multi-dimensional experience.

You asked friends from other universes, "Hey Frank, hold onto this magic and do not give it back to me no matter what I say." You gave away parts and pieces of you so you could come here and be embodied in these lower level frequencies as a way to become a master of this universe. You wanted to master experiences of this reality.

You knew you could never master things like pain and/or abuse if you were being the magic you truly be. You may identify with things like pain and/or abuse as a negative thing, when in reality it's all just experience. There is no right and wrong, no good or bad, just experience. I know this may bring a lot up for you and I completely understand. Just be present with me as we look at things differently. After all that is the key to change. Keep an open mind as you go through these concepts and allow yourself to expand beyond the emotional upset.

As we continue through this story you'll be diving into different concepts that will help you shift your perception of this reality. As you shift this will allow more of who you be to become present in this reality.

Before the shift of 2012, the frequencies were not high enough for us to embody anymore than about ten percent of who you are. This allowed for you to be integrated into many systems of limitations, lots of structures of polarity (right and wrong) and constructs that have kept you limited. It has also allowed for large scale manipulations of your body and your being. It has separated you deeply from the core of who you are.

Since the shift, you have been experiencing a global awakening. What we are all experiencing is a breakdown of matrix systems polarity (right and wrong), systems of limitations, and integration of truth and wholeness. This is a process that is naturally occurring. The more of the matrix system you break down, the more you clear the structures and constructs, the more of you that becomes present in this reality. As you become more present, more of your being is able to show up. When more of your being shows up, life gets easier and way better.

How much of you is present in this reality?

As we continue on it's important to understand that many of the things you have done, choices you have made and experiences you have had are directly related to how much of you has been present here in this reality.

If you can really understand that it's not that you're stupid or bad and wrong that you have gotten yourself in situations that don't work for you. At the core it's really that not enough of who you be has been allowed to be present. You literally have been so limited you have made choices, decisions and taken paths for your life that you just really had no awareness about.

Let's look at that now.

EXERCISE

Read this aloud:
"Truth as of today, what percent of me am I currently showing up as in this reality? More than twenty percent? Or less than twenty percent?"

Take a deep breath. Can you feel that?

Ask again:
"Truth as of today, what percent of me am I currently showing up as in this reality? More than twenty percent? Or less than twenty percent?"

Really allow yourself to perceive what feels true there.
Take some deep breaths and allow.

Surprising to even consider that you could be functioning in this world at less than twenty percent, but you are! Finding out you are functioning at less than twenty percent of who you be can be a bit disheartening, but that's totally by design. You had to show up at a small percentage of you in order to play in this reality.

Have you ever hear the stories of the GODS who were bored in heaven having everything they ever required at their fingertips? They asked to be able to go to the town and experience what life was like as a peasant. Then they forgot they were gods and they were limitless? Yes. That is what I am talking about.

You are an infinite being.

You came here to have an infinite experience and you have forgotten that you are really limitless!

Now is the time for you to awaken!

You have multi-layers of agreements, lifetimes of oaths and vows, points of views and belief systems that are currently keeping you in line with limitation.

You have been here in this universe for potentially hundreds of lifetimes. You get this isn't your first rodeo right? It took many reincarnations in order to be able to get to the level of master that you are showing up as now.

I know you may be thinking. "I am not a master. I am struggling over here." But the truth is you are a master. You are just caught in a fraction of who you be.

This universe is currently experiencing a global awakening. An awakening you have a part in. You are aware you came here to do something great. Now is the time to dive in, release, shift, and change. Time to reclaim who you be!

Everything you have been desiring is now possible!

Everything you know you should be able to do is coming!

This process will unlock and reintegrate the space of who you be, as the infinite being you be, and allow you to add more of you on a daily basis.

Now is the time to awaken and empower you as the infinite being you be!

Getting clear about who you are

Do you know that you are an infinite being?

What does that even mean?

You are an infinite amount of energy, of space and of consciousness.

This infinite space is your being.

You are an infinite being with a body.

This body is inside of your infinite being space.

When your body dies you will still be infinite energy, space, and consciousness.

The old idea that you are a body, and you exist within the body have greatly limited the true space of who we are. At one time we may have existed within the body but this way of thinking keeps us small.

The reality is you are a space as big as the pie we discussed earlier. Within this space of you are all the ideas, viewpoints, beliefs, commitments, debts and everything you ever agreed to.

The space of your being is actually your very own universe, which is creating the way your life is showing up.

I like to visualize it like this:

Your infinite being is a very large garden.

Your body is within the garden.

This garden has all your viewpoints, belief systems, commitments, agreements and so on, all planted within your garden.

Let's start with a viewpoint we can all identify with, "money is hard." You were first told this viewpoint energetically at a very young age.

- You grew up watching your parents argue and struggle with money.
- You witnessed relatives having money upset.
- Your teachers, your friends, their parents, everyone had some sort of money worry, stress, or idea.

Every time you were around these "worries, thoughts, ideas" you planted those as seeds.

The more times you were around the "worries, thoughts, ideas" the more seeds you planted.

Every time the "worry, thought, idea" was validated, you watered the seed.

Eventually you had your very own patch of "money is hard."

From there the universe responds, allowing you harvest what you planted.

You start creating a life where "money is hard."

Now this may not even be your thought, but because you planted it and validated it so many times, watching others struggle with it, it became an energetic imprint in your garden.

The universe does not care what you have energetically imprinted and planted in your energetic garden.

This universe is a frequency based experience.

If you have a big field of "money is hard" the universe will continue to bring you experiences to validate the what you have planted.

This universe does not care if you plant positive or negative viewpoints. It just responds accordingly.

Here's where it gets tricky for many of us. We have lifetimes upon lifetimes of energetic storage. Five lifetimes ago when you borrowed Earls cow Bessy, you promised him you would bring Bessy back. The next day you got hit by a train and your neighbor Phil takes Bessy for his own, you still owe Earl. You made a promise. You took something and never returned it. Karmically you still owe Earl. So there in your garden is the debt to Earl. This promise to return is there holding space.

This lifetime, you meet "Earl." Only now "Earl" is Carly. Carly comes into your life and you feel this overwhelming loyalty and friendship with Carly. One night Carly calls you and asks to borrow your car you just paid off. You let her because you just feel like you should. Carly never returns your car and totals it days later. That's how it works.

Every time you have ever promised, pinky sweared, made a pact or oath, agreement, commitment, and swore to God, you created a debt. These "debts" are stored in your garden.

Over the past one hundred lifetimes you have been around, you married approximately seventy-seven times. Each time you vowed till death do you part, in sickness and in health, you created a space for forever in your field. As an infinite being, do you ever die?

You are an infinite being, your being never dies. Your body dies.

As an infinite being who never dies you have three hundred ninety four agreements, oaths, vows, and commitments to one hundred and twenty-seven people, all stored within your garden.

Twenty-four lifetimes ago when you had a small house in a small village living comfortably with your family. You went to help out in the village and came home to discover that your family had been slaughtered and there were squatters were in your home. They had taken possession of your home and all your things. You were overcome with grief and you vowed to never have anything of value again. By doing so you invoked energy to be sure that you never had anything of value again. And today you wonder why you can never create value in your life.

You may have been born into a family who struggles with fear. You too will struggle with fear, for fear is just energy you store energetically.

When you see someone you love harboring these energies you see them as a value. Well, if my mom has a big patch of grief she must really like it, so I should have one too. You plant this energy and continue to recycle it, not understanding why and resisting it constantly with words like, "why is this happening to me?" Each time you validate it, you create it stronger and stronger. Each time you ask why you invite the universe to create it stronger as the universe is showing you the why.

When you can look objectively at everything you are experiencing in your life now, without it being right or wrong. You can see there could be a reason or some sort of value you once had for what you are experiencing.

Every concept you are tangled in is present for some reason.

The key to change, and truly releasing yourself from anything, is to release the "polarity"of it. The places and spaces where you are making what you are currently experiencing as right or wrong. You are experiencing it for some reason. Release yourself from the viewpoints of it and that will give you the space to change it.

In this book you will find tips and tools to easily release yourself from the stories that are sticking you. Let's go together to release yourself from the parts and pieces you no longer desire, surrendering, releasing and understanding every experience you have had has a reason and justification. Now to untangle yourself and release it for good!

Why being an empath is such a gift

You are an empath.

Are you aware of what that is or what it means?

When I ask people what they think about being an empath, the answers aren't generally very exciting.
It's generally many reasons why they hate being so aware.
"It's hard."
"It's draining."
"I get caught in people's negativity."
"I take on other peoples stuff so deeply."

I have really yet to talk to one person who is excited or has joy in the fact that they are an empath. You are also empathic. Defined as
defined as the psychological identification with the feelings, thoughts, and or attitudes of others.

If you get the garden idea, you can see that when you get close to someone's garden you can see and feel what they have planted there. There is no right or wrong, good or bad with what someone has planted. It's the way YOU perceive what they are going through that sticks you.

It's the idea that what they have planted or what they are experiencing is in some way shape or form not "right" or not "good."

Let me repeat that.

It's the idea that what they have planted or what they are experiencing is in some way shape or form not "right" or not "good."

It's the way YOU process THEIR information that sticks you with other people's stuff.

Your body is a receiving organ.
Your body is just receiving information.

That woman is angry.
That man is excited.
That child is sad.

It's your inquisitive energetic nature to get into what they are experiencing and try to figure it out and help them change it.

As an empath and an empathic person you can identify deeply with everyone's emotional upset. So deeply that you may actually even feel the same exact reaction in your own body. That is why being empathic feels so difficult. Their energetic garden magnetically impacts yours. Creating a similar emotional response without having the experience.

It is further engaged when you say things like, "why would someone do that?" Or "what were they thinking?"

When you ask questions about other people's situations you actually pull the information from their universe and invoke it your own.

You are a powerful creator. You are capable of creating anything you desire.

The key is to learn how to separate your thoughts from others and your energies from others.

When you can successfully identify who you are, what is yours and what you desire, you will then be able to see the true gift you are.

Here you will be able to access the true power of being the infinite being you truly be.

Being an empath gives you constant information. It feeds your desire for the information you came here to learn.

Now is the time to embrace the gift being an empath is and start living the true space of being an empathic all knowing being.

**You are a gift to this world.
Now is the time to embrace it and be it!**

Chapter Two
Tools you can use

Being present with your body

As we dive into these reality changing tools learning to be present with your body is very important.

Your body will be where you will be filtering information to create you as the aware being you be.

Learning to connect and be present with your body is essential.

One way to stay connected is through your breath.

You can control how your body reacts and responds by allowing yourself to slow down by focusing on breathing.

Next we will do a breathing exercise. Learning to connect to you through breath is very helpful in this journey.

EXERCISE

To start let's take some nice deep breaths.

Inhale counting to three, exhale counting to three.

Allow your tummy to fill with air and collapse.

Taking some nice deep breaths over and over.

Inhale 1-2-3, Exhale 1-2-3

As you do this allow your body to really be present with your breath.

Feeling your body slow down.

Feel the way your body feels at ease as you focus on your breath.

Inhaling 1-2-3, Exhaling 1-2-3

Connecting deeper and deeper to the slow down energy.

Inhaling 1-2-3, Exhaling 1-2-3

This is you. Your being has a slow and a low vibration. In this slow and low you will find the ease of connection to you. You will find that the following tools will work way greater if you are able to continuously connect to this space of you. The slow and low of who you be.

When you feel anxious.
Breath.
Inhale 1-2-3, exhale 1-2-3.

Anytime you feel overwhelmed or in upset, connect to your breath and use some of the tools provided in this chapter.

Nothing is as effective as connecting to your body through breath.

We will refer to breathing as the number one tool, the second tool would be expanding, which is next. Beyond that the rest of the tools are interchangeable and situational.

Please do not judge yourself through the process of learning the rest of these tools. I am providing lots of space in this book so you may digest and slowly learn these life changing processes. Stay out of your head. Relax as much as possible. The following pages offer a new way to exist in this world. Give yourself time and space to ingest it.

Stop protecting yourself and start expanding

Tool number two is expanding.

Are you still putting walls and or bubbles of protection around yourself? I too believed that I had to protect myself daily. I believed that if I didn't protect myself something terrible would happen or someone would hurt me.

What I have learned is protecting yourself is limiting your life. When you put up walls of protection all you are doing is stopping yourself from receiving information and locking yourself into the current contractions of your reality.

You are a receiver.

Your body is a receiving organ always receiving information from everyone and everything. Your body's here to give you information all the time. When you "protect" yourself, what you are doing is stopping the flow of information. You are literally cutting yourself off from the information the world is giving you. When you protect yourself from "bad things" you are actually stopping yourself from receiving the information, therefore, blocking your awareness. You want to become the receiver. Allow yourself to know everything there is to know.

Have you ever had someone do something to you like take advantage of you? And your response may have been, "I had no idea they were capable of doing that." Well, the reason you had no idea they were capable of that is that at some point you protected yourself from the information. Therefore allowing the very thing you were protecting yourself from to enter your life.

It's like you put up walls in front of your face guarding you against the energy of that, but in reality, all you did was put on a blindfold.

If someone is capable of taking advantage of you, you want to know. You don't want to "protect" yourself from it. You want to see it, feel it, know it so strong in your gut so you can choose not to be around them. You want to have a choice.

My oldest daughter went to Chicago last year for college. I wanted her to be armed with her awareness, not protection. So I taught her how to expand, receive information and acknowledge what she received.

You want to know who people are and what they are capable of doing. Because let's face it, if you know someone is capable of kidnapping you, aren't you more apt to make a better decision in their presence? If you know someone is capable of molesting children, are you going to leave your kids alone with them?

Now is the time to stop protecting yourself and start being aware of everyone and everything.

There is no fear in the known, fear can only reside in the unknown. Time to know.

Stay expanded and receive everything

Learning to expand your being is a great way to "protect yourself" without protecting yourself! When you expand you make the molecules of your being larger. By doing this you basically create everything going through your being. No energies get stuck. You then have awareness and information of everyone and everything. Let's learn how now.

You are a being.
You have a body.
Your body is within your being, your being is not inside of your body.

You are an infinite amount of energy, space and of consciousness.

It's time to learn how to harness the true space you be by allowing yourself to take up all the space you are.

When you expand, you give your being more space. You also give yourself more room to be you. Expanding is a simple exercise that when done often will create more space for you, reduce the time you spend in frustration and allow you to easily access what you know.

Expanding is an exercise, the more you do it the better you become at it. The more time you spend in expansion the more aware you will become in the expanded space.

EXERCISE

Step one:
Take some nice deep breaths. Inhale 1-2-3. Exhale 1-2-3.

Put your barriers down... barriers all the way down.

Repeat out loud: barriers down, barriers down, barriers down as you feel the barriers around your body melting.

Give yourself space and allowance in the safety and comfort of your home.
No need for protection.
All of the barriers all the way down.
Continuing to take nice deep breathes. Inhale 1-2-3. Exhale 1-2-3.

Step two:

Allow your being to expand, not your body.

As we go through this verbal exercise say each step out loud.

No need to visualize or even stay present with your being, just speak the words below out loud and know that your being will be expanding.

Your being knows how to expand and will continue to do so as it follows your verbal cues.

Take some deep breaths in and out. Inhale 1-2-3. Exhale 1-2-3.

Step three:

Give your being not your body these verbal cues:

"Expand out as big as the room I am in, go all the way down as much as it is wide and all the way up." Deep breath and relax.

"Expand out as big as the building I am in, going all the way down as much as it is wide and all the way up." Deep breath and relax.

"Expand out as big as the block I am on, going all the way down as much as it is wide and all the way up." Deep breath and relax.

"Expand out as big as the city I am in, going all the way down as much as it is wide and all the way up." Deep breath and relax.

"Expand out as big as the county I am in, going all the way down as much as it is wide and all the way up." Deep breath and relax.

"Expand out as big as the state I am in, going all the way down as much as it is wide and all the way up." Deep breath and relax.

"Expand out as big as the country I am in, going all the way down as much as it is wide and all the way up." Deep breath and relax.

"Expand out as big as the planet we are all on, as big as planet earth. Becoming one with everyone and everything. Bigger and faster and bigger and faster." Taking some nice deep breaths allowing your being to assimilate to the new space.

"Expand out as big as the universe we are in, bigger and faster, taking up all the space of the universe." Pause "The multiverse multiple universes." Pause "Times that by a million. Times that by a million. All the way out to the space of who I be as the infinite being I be."

Breathing. Relaxing. Settling into the space of you. Nice deep breath.

You are an infinite being with an infinite amount of energy, space and consciousness.

When you first start expanding you may not really feel any different and that's okay. The more you practice the better you get and the further you go. Initially expanding out several times a day is ideal, making sure you're taking lots of breaks to be present with your breath. The more you do this the more space your being will take up and the more space you will become used too. The more space you stay in the more you will see the emotional upsets fade out and more space for possibilities will become available.

What if you could just remove the stuff that bothers you?

What if you could clear yourself from thoughts and feelings you don't like?

What if you could change the way you feel about your past and your future?

What if you had the power to be able to release and remove anything that upset you or made you feel bad, whether it was thoughts, feelings and/or emotions?

What if you could be super magical with yourself and your universe?

What if you really truly did get to decide what you want to be in your life and what you don't?

Taking what we have discussed thus far, you are an energetic being. Understanding that you have a garden full of energy creating the way your life is showing up. What if you could just change it?

**It's your universe, you get to decide.
It's your garden and your choice to weed it.**

**This is an ask and receive universe.
You are in control of what goes on in your universe.**

You are a powerful creator capable of creating massive waves of change throughout your life.

It's your universe and you get to decide what is going on in it.

If there is stuff you don't like, you can change it. If something feels painful and upsetting, you can change it. So how do you do that? Well, at the core of it is choice. It's the awareness that no matter what you have going on you can choose to change it. You may have lots of things in your life you hate or dislike. But you are the only one that has the power to change it. Looking at what we have already learned, understanding that it's all just energy, you can use that to choose to release it and create something different. Let's move forward into really choosing to change the energy in your field with choice and a magical tool I use often.

Now I am going to share with you a magical tool to help create releasing and removing fast and easy. This is one of my favorite tools beyond choice, that you can use to choose to clear something from your universe and remove it for good. It's very simple and very effective at creating a change of energy in your space. It's an action that solidifies an active choice. It's called vaporizing.

Example: I am aware I am functioning in anger and I really don't want to be angry anymore. Using my power of choice, I am going to choose to remove all the places and spaces anger is stored and I am going to choose to remove it all right now, (active choice) and then I am going to vaporize it. The vaporizing is kind of like a solidifying tool. It solidifies that you asked to remove the energy and the play of it helps to actively create the change. Let's practice!

EXERCISE

Take something that is currently bothering you, it can be a thought or an image of something.

Bring it up and allow it to come into your awareness. Maybe it is something you said today? Or maybe it is something someone else said? Maybe it is a feeling that you can't shake. Or an emotional upset that is really plaguing you.

Say, "Everything all of that is, I choose to remove and release all of it from my universe and I choose this now."
Then say, "Vaporize, vaporize, vaporize."

You can move your arms around clearing it. Or you can envision like a fire extinguisher clearing it out of your space. Or you can just say that and not do any action.

Let's feel that space again. Does it feel different? Is there still that same nagging feeling? Let's go in some more.
Say, "Everything all of that is, I choose to remove and release all of it from my universe and I choose this now."
Then, "Vaporize, vaporize, vaporize."

Go back to that space now. Can you perceive the difference?

This is your universe, you get to decide what energies are in it. And if you decide to remove something, you can.

No one or nothing can stop you. You are a infinite being with infinite choice. If you choose to remove something from your energy field, you get to. There really isn't any right or wrong and the energy of play with it helps to expand the space even greater.

Releasing and removing energy in this way will create a difference in your energy, space and consciousness. It will also create your life showing up differently.

The thing is when you start choosing to be different, actively calling out what you want to remove and then clearing it out of your field, you can expect massive change.

This clearing may seem weird for you at first, I totally get it! It is a bit out there, but let me tell you what, it actually really truly works to change the energy in your life!

Number one, it's based on your choice. This is the most important thing to understand. Your choice creates.

Number two, you are giving the universe an active tool to help release and remove the stuff you no longer like! How awesome is that?

It's really a pretty cool tool that you always have with you.

Whenever you say something and you think, "why in the world did I say that?" Follow that up with, "Everything all of that is I choose to remove and release that from my universe, vaporize" When you actively start calling out stuff you no longer like, you choose to remove it and vaporize it, you will notice huge changes in your life.

And the best part? You cannot, I repeat cannot cause something bad to happen by choosing and vaporizing. You will not remove something you need later, because the reality is, you always still have choice. The only thing we are doing with the vaporizing tool is releasing and removing the places and energetic spaces where you don't have choice. Releasing and removing the places and spaces that feel uncomfortable or upsetting.

But the thing is, if it comes back around and you decide you want it back even though you vaporized it out before, you can absolutely still choose it! Mostly what we are doing with the vaporizing is creating new space for you to do something different and have new choices.

As we discussed before, much of your field is planted with solidified view points. When you clear it, you get to plant whatever you would like! And if you plant something and decide the next day or next week or next month you don't like that anymore, guess what? You can choose to remove and release it and vaporize it out of there and start again! There is really no wrong choice. It's all just choices! As you play with this tool more you will see first hand how very powerful it can be. Let's do some together! Let's deep dive into the stuff that is creating your reality and release what no longer works for you.

Clearing out your garden

Let's get clear about what you have stored, at least what you have conscious knowledge of now. As you go through this process you will be creating space for the stuff underneath to get clear as well. It's kind of like an onion. You are going to start peeling the layers away of what you know now. The more you dive in, the clearer you get, the easier this process becomes.

This is a life altering process.

Each and every time you choose to go through your past and actively change it energetically, you will create massive shifts and changes in your life.

Becoming aware of your thought patterns is key to change. This process maybe difficult at first but it will be so worth it!

What is it that you have planted in your garden?

EXERCISE

Grab some paper and a pen and let's get clear about what energies you are recycling.
- Write three recurring thoughts.
- Write three things you continuously worry about.
- Write three things that your parents said to you when you were young that you still hear in your head.
- Write three things that someone has said to you in the past that still bother you today.
- Write three things you are fearful of happening.

After you have completed the exercise, take each one of your thoughts and ask:
- Is it true?
- Does it contribute to my life?
- Is it worth continuing?

Now take that thought and state:
"Everything that this thought is, I choose to release and remove it from my universe and I choose that now" (your choice is key). Then, "Vaporize, vaporize, vaporize."

If you don't like vaporize you can say or do something different. There is no right or wrong here. It's really about your intention to release and remove it.

The point of this exercise is to become aware of what energies you have stored in your field. The thoughts you are continually looping in are the thoughts that make up your energetic space. Use this exercise to not only become aware of the thoughts but to really change them. This exercise will give you space to release, untangle and unwind those thoughts so you may have a different possibility.

It's your universe, you get to decide.

All of these thoughts exist because you have given them space to exist. Now you are aware they are there, you get to choose to remove them.

This is your universe. This is your life.

You get to decide what thoughts and emotions you have stored as real and true, and you get to control what is cycling in your head. Right now choose to release them.

Let's even go a step further and look at the energy that exists within some of these things you have been cycling in.

Your three recurring thoughts

These thoughts are based on past experiences. They actually have absolutely nothing to do with the current moment.

Why do you loop in them? Your brain "needs" something to do. Your brains' job is to store information and have it available for when you require it. Your brain can only comprehend the information it already has experienced. Your brain can't process things outside of what it already has experienced or learned. Your brain cannot bring in new information only your body can.

Keeping that in mind, you have to learn how to allow the brain to have thoughts without storing them as true and without engaging within it. It's like having a conversation with someone who isn't listening. Allow your brain to talk to you without paying attention. Learn to get into your body without engaging in the head noise. We will be diving deeper into this concept soon. Essentially you want to learn not to pay attention to the looping thoughts. They are just playing for the brain. Once you stop engaging them they stop occurring.

Three things you continuously "worry" about

When you worry, you are actually worshipping that thought. Most of our worries are things that when we actually look at them aren't as scary as we think. Let's take one of those worries. If that worry happened, what would be created? Like let's take a big one people often worry about, money. "What if I don't have enough money to pay my bills."

Have you ever not had enough money to pay your bills? Or did you always pull it off? More than likely you always pulled it off.

And if you say, "well one time I had to claim bankruptcy because I didn't have enough money." Ok, so? Did you die? Did your worst nightmare come true? Or did you come out the other side to tell the story?

Let's just say, you did have something happen like you ran out of money and you had to move. Is where you're at now better? Or worse? What if what "happened" was exactly what you required? What did you learn? How have you grown?

Remembering you are here to play in various concepts, what if you created whatever happened because you're required to? One of the things I often like to remind myself of is the shift happened in 2012. We have way more power now then we ever have. You are now armed with more knowledge and more power than you have ever had. You do not ever have to be a victim to any circumstances.

This is your universe and you get to decide.

The faster you grasp the concept of what we are currently cycling through, the faster you can embrace and become the master of your universe. The easier it becomes to no longer be the effect of things "happening to you." You are in charge and you get to decide. Stop holding anymore space for things you do not want in your life. More than likely everything you are "worrying" about is not what you desire to create.

Get out of your head. Take a deep breath.

Ask yourself, "why am I worshipping this problem? Is this something I desire to create? Is this something I want my life to be like?" If that is not something you want to create, follow the these steps.

1. Actively choose to release and remove it.
"I choose to release and remove this thought from my universe and I choose this now. Vaporize, vaporize, vaporize."

2. Choose to stop engaging in the noise of it. Ignore the thoughts, eventually they will go away.

3. Find stuff that brings you joy! Start asking for the stuff that lights you up!

We will go over deep asking and receiving soon but keep that in your mind. What is fun for you? Worrying takes a ton of time and space so if you're totally committed to stopping the worry, you must find something to replace it with.

Three things that your parents said to you when you were young that you still hear in your head

Let's look at these thoughts. Most of these thoughts are probably not even thoughts that your parents had. These could be:
- thoughts they were fearful of creating.
- things people said to them.
- thoughts from their parents and or bloodline.
- recycled autoresponder thoughts.

They more than likely have absolutely nothing to do with you.
When someone says something to you over and over you start resisting and reacting to the thought. The more resistance you have to the thought the more power the thought has over you.

To change these thoughts, first choose to clear them and then surrender to the energy of them. The process of surrender is an easy process. It's the process of deeply realizing there is nothing you can do to change the past. Your parents did the best they could with the tools they had. Allowing the energy to stay with you only creates more upset for yourself.

Take a thought and repeat:
"Everything all of this is I choose to remove and release all of it from my universe and I choose that now. Vaporize, vaporize, vaporize."

Take some nice deep breaths. And allow yourself to relax and surrender into the energy.

You are a powerful creator capable of changing anything.

Nothing anyone has said about you has to continue to create your reality.

You get to decide who you want to be everyday.

No one knows more about who you are than you.

No one has the power to create you as something except you.

You are the only one who is capable of creating anything in your life.

Time to take your power back.

You are a powerful creator capable of creating anything you desire.

I understand first hand how difficult it can be to release that childhood pain. This next process will help you deeply release that pain so you can move forward feeling healed from your childhood trauma.

This is a process that not only heals you but also releases your parents and their thoughts as a projection of who you be. Remember you are an infinite being and you get to decide how your life is going to be.

This is your universe, you get to decide.

Take a time when your parents or parent said one of those thoughts that continues to bother you. If you can, envision yourself at that age. Often in our painful memories we can see the picture of ourselves.

If you look at that memory, are you seeing it from the vision of it happening to you, first person?

Or can you see it from the picture of what happened, second person?

I find it interesting that many of our painful memories are stored from a second person memory. It's as if you are watching it happen to a version of you, but you are not within the vision. That confirms to me how you store energy. You store it as an energetic picture. This picture or image of you, holds an energetic marker to pain from the past.

Do the following exercise to remove that painful past and give yourself space for something greater.

Let's change these thoughts for good!

EXERCISE

ENERGY PULLS

Before beginning be sure to get present with your body. Take some nice deep breaths 1-2-3. 1-2-3. Put your barriers down and expand.
You always want to be in an expanded place prior to pulling and receiving.

Get an image from your past and project it out in front of you.

Now pull pure positive life force energy from behind you and the situation. Like a huge wave of pure positive life force energy. Pull it through the situation and all the way through your body.

Keep pulling that energy through the space in between and now receive that energy into your current body. Pulling and receiving. Taking some nice deep breaths 1-2-3, 1-2-3.

Allow yourself to receive all this pure positive life force energy from the old situation. Pulling and receiving. Really being present with the moment. Breathing 1-2-3. 1-2-3.

Now as you continue to receive, from your arm pit area send back to you the energy of gratitude. Give the situation this gratitude, allowing every aspect of the situation to be immersed in gratitude from you.

Then pull that gratitude back, creating a gratitude cycle from the old you to the new you, filling both of you with gratitude. Being thankful and grateful for the experience you had. Grateful for the space of you. Thankful for the trials and tribulations of the past as these situations have taught you and allowed you to grow.

Continuing to pull and receive and be filled with gratitude.

> Continuing to breathe, feeling your body relaxing more and more with the space of ease.
>
> As you melt into this space feel how different you feel. How much more relaxed your body is, and how much more ease you are perceiving. Now release yourself and the situation. And take some nice deep breaths.

Now go back to that situation.

Do you feel how different it feels? Be with that space for a moment. Take a nice deep breath.

How much more relaxed is your body? Do you still feel the same nagging feeling? Is there more space for you? Or less space?

    If it still feels like there is any upset in there, do it again. You may also require to clear and receive from each parent the situation occurred. If you have a lot of upset with your father, start with him. You will want to use the same process but this time instead of the situation you want to put the person or people involved. Pull and receive from them and then implant the gratitude. We will be deeper diving into this process throughout the book.

    You can use this technique to go through any trauma you are holding onto. Use this as a gift for yourself and your parents. You will be amazed at how when you do this your relationship with them will change. You will no longer be functioning in upset with them, and they will be so much happier and nicer to you with no upset in between. We will be doing this pulling exercise often in the coming chapters. This exercise truly heals your life.

Write three things that someone has said to you in the past that still bother you today

Kind of the same concept as before. Really get clear about those things. Are those things actually true? Nothing ties us up more than a lie. When you find yourself in reaction to someone's words, more than likely those words are just not actually true for you. In this reality, what's true for you may not be true for me. What's true for me may not be true for you. It's based on their point of view from their understanding. It's not fact, it's viewed through their viewpoint. When you can acknowledge that something someone else said about you isn't true and its based upon their viewpoint it's easier to release.

You can also do some pulls to create more of a change. Do just as we did in the last exercise except put the situation in there. You will be amazed at how fast you can release this trauma. The more you pull the better you feel!

Three things you are fearful of happening

As you look at those things now with the information above can you already feel how those fears feel differently? Those fears are only based upon the brain's ability to create projections from other people or things that aren't true. Be clear with your fears.

Are they required?

Can you just release them?

Is it possible you can just release and remove them? If so, choose to do that now.

It's time to stop living in energies that are not serving you and move into who you be, an empowered, awakened, infinite being.

As we continue on, we will be doing lots of different processes to clear, change, shift and transform our gardens. We just started with becoming aware. We will also grab, shift, change, and or clear certain energies. This is a huge process. There will be lots more learning involved.

As you continue to process energy you may feel foggy, unclear, and even a bit strange. Clearing your energy, space and consciousness in this way creates ripples of change in your life. These ripples can be wearing at times. Please be gentle with yourself. Reach out for help when you feel overwhelmed. And remember, you are an infinite being with infinite choice. Don't buy into anything that doesn't expand you.

I am also sharing another clearing that can help push you through the fog. This clearing is used specifically to just help clear in general.

Say aloud:
"All the SHICUUUU, stupidity, unconsciousness, anti consciousness energy fog around all of this, I choose to remove from my universe. Vaporize, vaporize, vaporize."

This statement means:
SHICUUUU: all of the secret, hidden, invisible, covert, unseen, unsaid, unacknowledged, undisclosed, and unconscious energies.
Stupidity: all the energy making you stupid or keeping you from your truth.

Unconsciousness: all the energy that you are not conscious of.
Anti-consciousness: all the energy that you are using against consciousness.
Energy fog: anything that is creating you feeling unclear.
Alternatively you can say:
"Universe I am choosing to remove all the SHICUUUU, stupidity, unconscious, anti-conscious, and energy fog around all of this and I choose this now, vaporize"

You cannot do this clearing wrong. The goal is to remove everything in the way of you getting clear.

As we continue on you will be learning many more tools you can use to help you on this journey.

Your body is a receiving organ

Your body is a receiving organ that receives information from the world around you.

Your mouth tastes.

Your nose smells.

Your eyes see.

Your ears hear.

Your skin feels.

Your body is continuously receiving information from everyone and everything.

Your brain is your body's information center. Your brain is taught how to process the information by what you have learned in your life. Your senses take in information and your brain identifies the information. If the information is unknown, your brain dumps the information and allows your body to bypass whatever the unknown is. Your brain cannot comprehend things it does not already know. You can teach your brain things through integrating your senses, but if the information is unknown the brain cannot process it.

This is best described in the story of when Christopher Columbus first came to America. The story says that only the Shamans, the spiritual leaders, were able to see the ships approaching the shore. They didn't know what the ships were but their awareness was expanded enough to be able to "see" something approaching land.

The Indians, however, couldn't process the ships because it was so far outside of what they perceived to be true. They say the pilgrims were on land for days before the Indians even saw them.

This is the same for us. Our brain is only capable of "seeing" what it believes to be true or what it has received in the past. Have you ever "seen" something you never "seen" before? Maybe it's a new home on your route to work? Or a new road sign on your drive home. The first time you see these things you think, "Is that a new house? Couldn't be. Its old and looks like those around it. Why have a never "seen" it before?" Could be lots of reasons why you never seen it, but more then likely it was a processing issue. Something about the home or road sign you were not able to process.

Starting now you will be giving your body the space to become the true receiving organ. This book will teach you step by step on how to allow your body to process information outside of what it believes to be true. This is a process that is life changing. Learning to be a receiver changes your life dramatically.

How you do that is to start asking questions and receiving the information. This is called asking and receiving. When you ask and receive it's important to not listen to the information your brain tells you, allow your body to receive the information. No head answers only body sensations.

When you start asking and receiving you give your body new space to become a true receiver. This allows you to shift out of the old paradigms of thinking.

We live in an ask and receive universe.

Universal law states:
Ask and you shall receive.

Asking and receiving can become
a way of life.

There is no need to struggle in an
ask and receive universe.

If you can receive the information
you can actualize anything.

There is nothing you can not be, do or have
when asking and receiving.

Everything you desire is within reach.

Ask to receive.

EXERCISE

Start by taking some nice deep breaths. Inhale 1-2-3. Exhale 1-2-3. Really get present with your body. Breathing 1-2-3. 1-2-3.

Put your barriers down, barriers down, barriers down and let's expand out.
Expand out as big as the building you are in, all the way out, all the way down and all the way up.

Expand out as big as the county you are in, all the way out, all the way down and all the way up.

Expand out as big as the state you are in, all the way out, all the way down and all the way up.

Expand out as big as the country you are in, all the way out, all the way down and all the way up.

Expand out as big as the planet we are on, as big as planet Earth, breathing, allowing, shifting, expanding all the way out, all the way down and all the way up. Bigger and faster. Nothing is stopping you.

Expand out as big as the universe, all the way out, as big as the universe actually is, and into the multiverse. Multiple universes. And times that by a million, times that by a million and time that by a million. Really getting all the way into the space of who you be as the infinite being you be.

As you get comfy in this space we will start asking and receiving.

What we will do is ask a question, pause and allow the information to come into your body. Allow the information to come into your body paying attention to where the information enters.

Take a nice deep breath and let's ask the first question:

"What can I receive to live a life beyond my wildest dreams?"

Take a deep breath and receive. Allow this information to enter your body.

In a moment you will ask the question again, only this time you will completely stay out of your head. Your head does not know the answer to this question, if it did you would be living a life way greater than you do now. You are not looking for a head answer. You are allowing your body to receive information from the universe for your unique frequency. Keep breathing and stay present here.

When you ask a question of the universe, the universe responds energetically to your frequency.

Your body energetically receives the information.

When that information comes into your body it does not "sound" like anything.

It's responding with the energy you would require to make that happen. Depending on the depth of the question really depends on how many times you would have to ask and receive to become that space.

Asking a question like the one above, is potentially a far out question, because you have absolutely no awareness as to what it would take to live a life beyond your wildest dreams. You may not even have awareness of what your wildest dreams are yet! So asking and receiving with this question is purely energetic.

It's really amazing to me how people change when they learn these tools. They discover that the lonely yearning inside of them, they always felt, was really the yearning of who they are. This reality has not taught us how to be connected to who we are and what we love. This process of asking and receiving allows us to connect to our unique frequency and vibration by asking and receiving from the universe.

Let's ask the big question again:
"What can I receive to live a life beyond my wildest dreams?"

Sit with that energy.

Do you feel a rush of information come into your body?

Where do you feel it at?

Its ok if you don't feel anything yet. It's normal to not really be feeling anything.

No one has taught you how to receive.

As we continue on and you practice, you will see how very easy being a receiver really is. It's like a muscle, the more you do it, the less you engage in your head, the easier it becomes.

What you want to look at now is, where is your body receiving the information?

Are you receiving information in through your eyes?

Let's ask and pay attention to if you can feel the information coming into your body anywhere.

Try asking this question:

"What can I receive today to have receiving be ease right away?"

Pause, take a nice deep breath, no head noise. Ask again.

"What can I receive today to have receiving be ease right away?"

What you maybe experiencing is a slight rush of energy that you may or may not feel. Here are some signs your body is truly receiving.

- Right after asking the question you take a nice deep breath. That deep inhale means your body IS receiving information.
- Your body feels more relaxed. There is a "feeling" going on inside your body that feels very peaceful.
- You may feel a slight rocking or vortexing inside your body. This feeling maybe like rocking or spinning.

These are some common signs that you are in fact receiving. You may have some or all of these signs or you may have something different. Let's look at did you feel the information entering your body?

Remember this information does not sound like anything. You want to feel the information come into your body. You also want to be sure the information is not entering into your head. You want the information to come through your heart space.

Let's ask again:

"What can I receive today to have receiving be ease right away?"

Pause, take a nice deep breath, no head noise. Ask again.

"What can I receive today to have receiving be ease right away?"

Are you feeling the information come in anywhere? If you were feeling it in your eyes or into your head, you want to shift it down into your heart space. Your head filters the information, your heart is pure and allows the information to be actualized into the body.

If you aren't feeling it come in that okay! It does take lots of practice to really get into being a receiver. Main thing is that you stay out of your head with the answer and you have the intention that your body is receiving the information.

Your body is a receiving organ capable of receiving information about anything you desire.

Let's try it again, this time asking the question and lightly tap your hand on your heart area as to allow the information to be received there.

Tapping your heart space
Ask out loud:

"What can I receive today to have receiving be ease right away?"

Pause, tapping your heart space, no head noise, allow yourself to feel the expansion. Nice deep breath.

And one more time:

"What can I receive today to have receiving be ease right away?"

Pause, tapping your heart space, no head noise, allow yourself to feel the expansion.

We will continue to play with this in future chapters. The goal is to shift into asking questions about everything and allowing your body to receive the information. Please use the following pages as a guide to asking and receiving.

Asking questions to actualize anything

If you can receive it, you can actualize it! Every question you ask of the universe has an energetic response. As we continue in this awakened journey, we will be integrating more and more questions.

The more you ask questions about something the easier it is to actualize the space of it.

It goes back to the garden analogy. If you keep planting the seeds of what it is you desire, eventually you will actualize exactly what it is you are looking to create.

Right now we are going to start with some simple ask and receive questions.

When you ask a question, the universe has an energetic response.

Let's start by asking this:

"What can I receive to allow my body to guide me with ease?" And just receive. No head noise. Take a deep breath. Allow the energy to be received throughout your body.

No head noise. Pat your heart space. Receive and ask again.

"What can I receive to allow my body to guide me with ease?"

Take a nice deep breath and just really feel that energy go streaming into your body.

If you are having head noise, just allow it to play without reaction. If you try to stop the head noise it will get louder and stronger. You want to just acknowledge the head noise and move forward.

Let's ask that question again:

"What can I receive to allow my body to guide me with ease?" Touch your heart space and say receive.

Take a deep breath and just allow yourself to receive that information.

The more you ask the same question, the more information you will receive. The more you receive, the faster you become the space of the information.

One more time:

"What can I receive to allow my body to guide me with ease?"

Can you perceive all that expansive information coming your way?
Keep practicing!

The more you ask the more you receive!

When asking you want to stay with questions that are unbiased questions that expand your being. Use the questions on the next page as a guide to practice and create your own questions.

What can I receive to have
everything I desire with ease?

What can I receive to actualize a
life that works for me with ease?

What can I choose today to create
more ease in my life right away?

What can I choose to have
what I desire with ease?

What can I do or be to have
everything work out for me with ease?

What can I do or be to create
a life that expands me with ease?

What would it take to create
my dreams as reality with ease?

What would it take to create and
generate my dream life with ease?
What would it be like to have
everything I desire for all eternity?

Feeling your truth

You can learn to walk your truth by learning to feel what is true for you in your body.

Your body is a receiving organ capable of giving you information about everything you would like to do or choose.

Your body is very intuitive and is more than capable of giving you the answer to anything and everything you would like to know.

Knowing how to feel your truth is key to awakening and empowering yourself. Each one of us has our own truth and our own path.

What's true for you will always have a lightness, what's false for you will always have a heaviness.

When you are becoming a feeler something to keep in mind is that what's true for me, may or may not be true for you. And what works for me, may not be what works for you.

When you learn to tap into your own truth and the information the universe has for you, you learn to live an empowered life that works for you.

To start "feeling" a life that works for you, you must learn to ask questions and "feel" the answers. Notice I did not say hear the answer. I said "feel." This is not word answers, this is body sensations. What's true for you will always be light and/or create an expansion of some sort, what's false for you will always be heavy and contractive.

Key here is learning to ask questions about your life and your choices and feeling a lightness or a heaviness on what you are asking about.

Some people will perceive light and heavy in their body, like for me, the lightness starts in my lower pelvis and goes up through my body and out the top of my head. When something is false for me, the heaviness goes down through my body. Other people will perceive a heaviness/contraction or lightness/expansion around their body or in an area in their body like their heart space or pelvis area.

Everyone perceives light and heavy differently. Let's ask your body to show you how you perceive what is light and what is heavy for your body.

Let's ask:

"Body what does lightness feel like for me?" Pause, receive.
"Body, what does heaviness feel like for me?" Pause, receive.

Take some deep breaths and let's ask again:
"Body what does lightness feel like for me?" Pause, receive.
"Body, what does heaviness feel like for me?" Pause, receive.

The answer is an energetic answer that you want to allow your body to feel. If you are not feeling anything yet, that's ok. It takes lots of practice and lots of presence in the body to be able to perceive your light and heavy, especially if you are a head tripper.

If you spend a lot of time "thinking" and "figuring out" this skill will take some time to master. This skill **cannot** be used in conjunction with your head. It must be used as a replacement for the head noise. The less viewpoints you have about this exercise the easier it is as well.

Let's ask some questions and see if you can "feel" things differently. We will ask some simple truth questions. These are questions you already know the answer to. Stay present with how these questions feel to your body. Do not answer these questions with your head. If your head responds, it's ok, just be in allowance of what you hear but do not "listen to it," just allow it to play. We are going with body sensations only!

Please ask both questions before you "feel" like you have an answer. Again, these questions you will be asking are questions you already know the answer to. You will be just "feeling" the questions within your body to get the awareness of what lightness feels like and what heaviness feels like. Saying truth in front of the question lets your body know that you are looking for what's true for you.

Before you ask your questions, let's check in with your body again and this time ask your body:

"Body, please assist me in feeling heavy and light within my body."

And ask:
"Truth, my body likes to drink water."
Pause, allow the feeling and breathe.
"Truth, my body likes to drink bleach."
Pause, allow the feeling and breathe.

Ask them again.
"Truth, my body likes to drink water." Pause, allow the feeling and breathe.
"Truth, my body likes to drink bleach." Pause, allow the feeling and breathe.

Obviously, your body should like to drink water, even if it isn't thirsty right now, bodies like water. But bodies should not like to drink bleach. Keep asking these two questions until you can perceive some kind of lightness or expansion and a tightening or a heaviness.

You may additionally play with questions like,
"Truth, my body is sitting."
"Truth, my body is standing."

You want to get a body awareness of what truth and lies feel like for your body. Keep playing with simple truths to see if you can get to the perception of heavy and light.

As we continue on we will be addressing asking questions and clearing more space for you to be able to "feel." As the clearer you become, the less you function in viewpoints the easier it becomes to perceive your light and heavy.

Learning to ask questions to feel light and heavy

This process will teach you to ask questions and perceive the energy in your body about anything and everything you need insight about.

Learning to be a feeler does take some time.

Key is to stay out of your head and get into your body.

You have to get used to asking yourself questions without following what your head tells you. You have to be present with your body and the information as you receive it.

In the last section we did ask some this or that questions. We did my body likes to drink water or my body likes to drink bleach. These are this or that questions. This or that questions always assume that the answer is this or that.

When you are playing with simple truths like sitting or standing just to start perceiving information it's fine to ask this or that questions. But if you are asking to get to the truth of something you are not sure about or do not know yet, you do not want to ask this or that questions.

You want to ask questions to receive the energy of awareness not to "decide" something you have already decided about.

Often people feel like they have this choice or that choice, because they feel like those are their only choices. But the reality is this universe is full of possibilities, many you may not be aware of!

Just like we were talking about before with the ask and receive, you want to still ask about your choices and perceive the lightness or heaviness but you don't want to decide what you are choosing.

There are two different ways to ask questions to get to what is true for you.

If you are trying to get to the truth of something you want to ask a direct question followed by "or something else."

Here are some examples on how to use this:

You are looking at making a choice about buying something.

Ask:

"Would it contribute to my life if I purchased this? Or something else?" What feels light there?

You are trying to figure something out.

Please stop trying to figure stuff out! Ask questions.

"Is it 'this that I have decided?' Or something else?"

If you get more of a lightness on something else ask more questions.

"Is it "this" or something else." If you are stumped ask and receive for more information.

You can ask for things like:

"What would it take to have the information I require with ease?"

"What can I receive to have the information I require with ease?"

"What can I do or be to have ease with this situation now please?"

Then leave it for a few moments or even days depending on what kind of choice you are making.

Stay out of your head and keep asking.

The key here is to start functioning in asking questions instead of deciding that you know the answers. Also if you get something else, stop looping in trying to make the first thing true! I would say 99 percent of the time if you are playing and replaying something you are "trying to figure out" you are not in the truth of it. Which is why you are continuing to loop in the issue. Stop looping. Put your barriers down, expand out and ask some questions about it.

Remember to ask the question you are looking for the answer to and then ask, "or something else."

Do not decide it has to be this thing or that thing. Find which one feels lighter, ask some more. If you get stuck do some ask and receiving.

If you are looking at making a choice and you want to see what is light for you, you want to ask differently.

You want to take whatever it is you are asking about and get into what the choice is going to create in your life.

Example:

You are wondering about a new job.

Ask, "If I choose this job what's it going to create in my life?"

"If I don't choose this job what's it going to create in my life?"

You want to avoid ever trying to figure anything out and you want to get into the energy of what something is going to create.

Every single choice you make creates an energy in your life.

If you choose something that your body or life does not desire you will "feel" bogged down and frustrated with your life.

If you choose something that your body and life do desire you will "feel" light, happy, and an expansion.

If you choose based on what it "feels" like you will see how easy it can be to make big choices for your life. There is really no upset or frustration when you follow what is light and true for you.
It will take some time and lots of practice.

You must be willing to follow the lightness even if in the beginning it doesn't feel very light, maybe it's just a pinch lighter. Choose that.

The more you make choices based on the lightness the more the lightness will move in.

Making choices based on heavy and light is a process and its like building muscles. The more you do it, the more you use it, the better it becomes.

Sometimes choosing from lightness doesn't make much sense. If you use your body for a guide to something lighter, I guarantee eventually it will make some sense.

If you are asking and receiving and not getting to any lightness, clear the viewpoints and ask about something else. You are more than likely functioning in too much solidified point of views or rights and wrongs about the subject you are asking about.

Over the years and throughout the weeding of my energetic garden my light and heavy has increased dramatically. So if you struggle with light and heavy, do not give up. This is a process that is like a muscle, the more you play with it, the more you trust yourself with the answers, the stronger your sensations become. The easier it is to perceive the information and the faster you can stand in your truth.

The universe will give you a heavy or light for everything you would like to know, and the universe will deliver energy for everything you would like to actualize. The key to receiving the answers is to get yourself free from all points of views you have to everything!

As we continue on this journey we will be continuing to dissipate the storage of your over planted energetic garden which will make receiving answers way easier and faster as well.

Pulling and receiving

As you embark on this journey, pulling and receiving will be one of the most important tools you will use.

You will use this to pull and receive from yourself, other people, places and things.

Pulling and receiving will help you heal, it will give you information and it will allow you to really expand your knowing.

You did do a few pulling and receiving exercises at the beginning of this chapter. Now let's dive deeper.

Pulling and receiving does not take from anyone or anything.

When you pull and receive all you are doing is taking pure positive life force energy and pulling it from behind, through someone or something, through the space in between, and receiving the energy into your body, pulling it straight out the other side.

You are not taking anything.
You are not keeping anything.
You are only pulling pure positive life force energy through, receiving it and releasing it.

What this does is it allows for any contractions, any pent up energy, and any emotional intensities to be received in totality. When people, places or things are stuck in something, when you pull and receive you give another possibility.

If someone is stuck in anger, when you pull and receive you take pure, positive life force energy and you fill them with it. You pull that anger all the way through and into you and all the way out. What that does is allows the person who felt angry to be heard, seen and felt. This alone helps people release. It does not take it from them though. If they still want to be stuck in anger, they can be. It does not "take" their anger. It allows them to be filled with pure positive life force energy giving them a new space to be able to choose something different. They can absolutely still choose it if they would like, but often this process is enough to have them 'feel' heard so they can release it and no longer have to hold onto it.

How often have you felt upset about something and felt as though everyone was ignoring you? No one cared that you were upset? Well when you pull and receive someones upset you energetically acknowledge their pain. This alone is so freeing!

Let's start by practicing this on ourselves. This is an amazing exercise to help you heal your relationship with yourself.

EXERCISE

Before you begin make sure to get present with your body. Taking nice deep breaths. Then put your barriers down and expand out. When ever you do a pulling exercise be sure you are expanded.

Take a past memory you have where you feel upset with yourself.
This could be a recent memory or a very distant memory. Take one that you often think about.

Once you have that memory of you, put who you were on that very day out in front of you.

Get the situation that happened and put all of that right out in front of you.

Pull pure positive life force energy from behind you and the situation. A huge wave of pure positive life force energy. Taking nice deep breaths.

Pull it through the situation and all the way through your body.

Keep pulling that energy through the space in between.
And receive that energy into your current body.

Pulling and receiving. Taking some nice deep breaths.

Allowing you to receive all this pure positive life force energy from the old situation and the old you. Pulling and receiving.

Taking nice deep breaths. Visualizing. Pulling and Receiving. Knowing that even if you can not "see" you, intention is creating this as a reality.

As you continue to receive, from your arm pit area send back to you the energy of gratitude.

Give the old space of you this gratitude, allowing the old you to be immersed in gratitude from the current you.

Then pull that gratitude back, creating a gratitude cycle from the old you to the current you, filling both of you with gratitude.

Being thankful and grateful for the experience you had.

Grateful for the space of you.

Thankful for the trials and tribulations of the past as these situations have taught you and allowed you to grow.

Continuing to pull and receive and be filled with gratitude.

Continue to focus on your breathing.

Feeling your body relaxing more and more with the space of ease.

As you melt into this space feel how different you feel.

Deeply feel how much more relaxed your body is and how much more ease you are perceiving.

Now release yourself and the situation.

And take some nice deep breaths.

Now go back to that situation.

Do you feel how different it feels?

How much more relaxed you are with what happened?

If it still feels like there is some upset in there, do it again.

Use this technique to go through any trauma you are holding onto. Use this as a gift for yourself. The more you pull and receive from yourself the more you will feel yourself changing.

As we move on in the book we will be using this same technique to change other relationships. Do this exercise for yourself as much as possible and watch who you think you are change.

**This is your universe and you get to decide.
If you decide you are healing and
releasing your trauma,
the universe responds creating it as so.**

No stress. No worries. Choose the healing.

Chapter 3
Healing your body and being

Expansion of who you be

As you go through this process you will notice your thoughts and the things around you will start changing.

The more effort you put into the process the faster you will notice the change.

Allow yourself to have a greater awareness of your thoughts.

Please know that everything you are having awareness about is leading you to freedom. Do not allow yourself to stay in feeling bad for who you have been, things you may have done, or things that were done to you.

Everything you are aware of is present to help you shift, change and release yourself. Stop resisting who you have been. Stop resisting what has happened to you in the past. Give yourself time and space to process through what has been present in your life and allow yourself to heal.

You did not create your life this way overnight and you will not heal overnight. This is a process.

The tools I share in this book will help lead you to greater awareness and expansion of you. The more you use them the more your life will expand.

Surrender the idea that
your life will never change.

You are an infinite
being with infinite choice.

You are capable of changing
everything that doesn't work.

You are capable of changing
everything you do not like.

Breathe.

Expand.

Be present with your body.

You got this.

Stop resisting what you know

Time to deeply realize that you are not bad and wrong.

You are just aware, you always have been.

Most of the things you are making wrong about yourself is part of how this reality controls you.

- This reality teaches you to describe things and then makes you wrong for describing them. This creates a resistance of your knowing and a separation of your very being.
- This reality tells you to give everyone the benefit of the doubt even when you are aware of what they are creating or will create. This sets you up for disappointment and upset.
- This reality tells you you're wrong when you do what's right for you. This teaches you to not follow what you know.

What that has created is a continuous looping system where you are always second guessing who you are and what you know. Time to surrender to the resistance.

Acknowledge what you know

Acknowledging what you know maybe one of the hardest parts of being aware. As a child, you weren't allowed to be aware. You were taught right and wrong and good and bad. You weren't taught to listen to your inner guidance. You weren't encouraged to really know anything outside of what this reality deemed as real and true. When you were confronted with people, places or things that made you feel uncomfortable or uneasy, you weren't taught to follow that. You had to stuff it down and do what was necessary even if it meant going against what you felt.

Now it's time to fire up that inner knowing. It's time to connect to that inner feeling of what you know. And it's time to really acknowledge that you do know way more than you ever give yourself credit for.

Go to a time when you were little and something scared you or made you very upset. What did you really know about that situation? And not what someone told you, what did you know?

What were you aware of?

Here's where it gets tangly for each and every one of us. We have been taught not to be judgmental right? Not to judge or make an assumption to what you may or may not know. But I say bull crap. You know a lot. You are aware. You knew something was off that very day. You knew that you did not want to be part of that situation whatever it may be and someone told you it was fine. You went against what you were aware of and you were forced to do something you weren't comfortable with. And that's where you learned to not be aware.

In these situations, you were taught over and over to not listen to what you knew.

Just do what someone said.

Over and over you are taught to just do what your told.

Don't question anything.

Don't ask why.

When in all reality you were aware of something and it wasn't good.

What was it?

Get it out right now and acknowledge what you knew.

Was the man someone wanted you to go with creepy?

Did you feel upset about having to enter a building?

What did you know?

Allowing yourself to know information does not make you a bad person.

It does not make you wrong.

It's time to stand in what you know even if it feels uncomfortable.

As you do this acknowledging it's like acknowledging everyone everywhere.

Acknowledge the creepy man at the grocery store.

Don't shy away from him or hide.

Stay expanded.

Acknowledge him.

Look at his face, yes I see you. I am aware that you are creepy and capable of doing bad things.

Don't make yourself wrong.

Don't acknowledge someone and then loop back into, "oh I'm just being mean. I don't know that for sure."

Yes, you do.

Everything is energy.

You are aware of the energy.

When your body gives you information about someone stop making it wrong!

Part of this process is realizing that just because you know something about someone doesn't mean you have to do anything with it.

    Just because I see someone who I know is a child molester, doesn't mean I have to run to the police and tell on him. One, I have no proof and two, all I really have to do is acknowledge it. You see by me acknowledging it, I bring attention to the fact that it's true. When I do that I allow the person to stand deeper in that energy, by doing so that creates more awareness.

    When more awareness is present it creates the person having a harder time hiding. Someone who is capable of molesting children, or has in the past, wants to hide. They don't want to be public with that information. When you acknowledge it you bring more energy to the truth.

Now if you're wrong and that person isn't actually capable of that, that's ok too. Because if it isn't true the energy will just fall off. If it's not true it won't stick.

Acknowledging doesn't mean that you're always searching out the bad guys. Acknowledge everyone!

Acknowledge the happy people, spreading joy!

This will only make them shine brighter. Acknowledge the lonely sad old women alone grocery shopping, this will bring more attention to the fact she is lonely and will help her shift it easier and maybe even create people coming to visit her.

You can also use the energy techniques to pull and receive from these people, creating more space and ease for them to shift anything they desire into ease.

I often pull from everyone. The old lady at the grocery store who appears sad and lonely. No one has received from in a long time, I pull and receive and she will have a new joy in her step.

The crying baby at the mall will be filled with ease and joy, creating ease and joy for everyone in the area!

Pulling and receiving from strangers allows them to be received from, which we really all require, but also gives them some new space to choose something greater.

Remember to continue to clear the places around acknowledgment where you are feeling stuck. This is your universe and you always get to decide so if something is going on you don't like, clear it.

Be aware of where you are not in allowance of you. If there is anywhere you are making you wrong, keep catching it. Don't loop in wrongness. You are learning a new way to be. Be gentle with you. Allow yourself to change.

As you continue untangling your awareness and you start acknowledging more and more what you knew you will find that you have always been aware.

Nothing you have ever wanted to say was a judgment.

It was your awareness.

You are NOT judgemental, YOU ARE AWARE!

Your body is a receiving organ, receiving information from everyone and everywhere all the time!

You are an amazing receiver.

As you continue to read through the following pages you will find that your awareness will grow and you will see how very aware you truly be.

What do I know about me I have never acknowledged?

What do you know about you that you have never acknowledged? Are you a great friend? Do you have a special skill with people you never allow yourself to see? Are you aware of how very amazing you truly are?

I know you don't even want to allow yourself to perceive that at all do you? You are so convinced that you are bad and wrong that you can't even allow yourself to even fathom that you may be amazing.

As an empath, you tend to like to see the good in others and the bad in yourself.

You take the energies you are aware of in other people, internalize them and make them yours.

You are very good at being aware.

You are very good at knowing information.

You are very good at identifying emotion.

And you are very good at storing everything you are aware of as real and true.

One of the things I have learned is you are showing up at such a small percentage of who you are that you often can't identify what is yours and what is someone else's.

You are so caught up in feelings, emotions, and experiences that don't belong to you that you have no idea who you are and how you process information.

The good news is, now you can change that. You can ask and receive for more awareness of who you be and for more of you to show up. My personal experience with myself and others is that once more of you shows up everything gets easier and better.

EXERCISE

Here is a series of questions designed to help you get more information about you and who you be.

These questions are ask and receive, reminding yourself not to "answer" the questions with your head but just allow your body to receive the information.

Be sure to start connected to your body, taking nice deep breaths. Go to your expanded place of who you be.

Ask and receive the following questions.

"What can I receive to become more of me with ease?" Pause, take a deep breathe and receive.

"What awareness can I receive about me to allow my truth to come to me with ease?" Pause, take a deep breathe and receive.

"What can me and my body be to have permission to access my truth with ease?" Pause, take a deep breathe and receive.

"What would it be like to always know my truth with ease?" Pause, take a deep breathe and receive.

"If I wasn't thinking, what awareness would I have?" Pause, take a deep breathe and receive.

"What would it take for me to have complete ease for all eternity?" Pause, take a deep breathe and receive.

Ask these questions repeatedly for the next three or four days. Stay out of your head. Get present with you and who you be.

What you will start to notice is this:
- You will start to have awarenesses about you and about your life.
- Things from your past will make more sense.
- Things will be easier than they ever have been.
- People will be nicer to you.
- It won't seem so overwhelming to be around people.
- Conversation will be easier and easier.
- You will not feel so angry or frustrated with you daily tasks.
- Life in general will be easier.
- Relationships will change.
- Where there was once emotional upset or overwhelm, it seems to have faded creating some real ease.
- You may enjoy life!
- You may enjoy being in public!
- You can interact with strangers and you won't want to poke your eyes out.

Mostly at this point you will be noticing your life is changing.

Acknowledge that. You have come a long way. You have done ALOT of processing. You are pretty amazing.

Stop caring what other people choose

Each one of us is on our own unique journey.

No one person's journey is more significant than the others.

We are all just here experiencing stuff!

Just as you are experiencing life, making choices from the information you have provided and creating life from the energy you have harvested, so are others.

When we "care' or get upset or become enraged or even think someone else's choices aren't good, right, wrong, or whatever. It's all just a place where we are actually resisting and or upholding space to put something amazing in our own life.

The thing is when you get upset over someone else's choices that is a call to action. Somewhere you are aligning, agreeing, resisting, reacting, defending for or against or being righteous for or against their choice. It actually has nothing to do with them it has to do with you and your stored viewpoints.

When you find yourself in judgment of someone else's choice the first thing to become aware of is:

"What is it about this that is creating me as _____"

Receive the information, then you are going to clear. No head noise!

"Everything that is upholding that I choose to remove all of that from my universe and I choose that now. Vaporize, vaporize, vaporize."

Clear the polarity. "Where is everywhere I am aligning and agreeing, resisting and reacting, defending for, defending against, righteous for and righteous against. Everything all of that is I choose to remove all of that from all of my universes. Vaporize, vaporize, vaporize."

When you do that, you are going to the place where you have planted the point of view that is causing the upset and choosing to change it for good!

This is your universe, YOUR GARDEN!

It is your choice what you choose to store here from this point forward. The more aware you are, the more you allow yourself to see where you are reacting, the faster and easier it becomes to shift and change this stuff.

If you are looking to live a life that works for you, an empowered, awakened one, you have to look at everywhere someone or something is taking you out of being present and aware.

The fastest way to become the creator of your own reality is to get a grip on where you are making someone else's choices important in your world. The fastest way to create your world is to stop getting wrapped up into anyone else's.

This is your universe, you get to decide.

Clearing your space of upset with someone else

Are you ready to release the frustration, anger or any type of upset you have with someone?

Let's do some pulls you can use with anyone in your life at any time to reduce the energy that exists between the two of you.

Everything is changeable.

Everything.

Your point of view creates your reality, your reality does not create your point of view.

If there is tension or upset with anyone you can change that magically.

EXERCISE

Start by connecting to your breath 1-2-3. 1-2-3.
Put your barriers down and expand all the way out.

Put a memory of a person that you have some sort of upset with.

Really get the energy of that person and the situation.

Bring forward everything you feel.

Now imagine that person is out in front of you.
From here you are going to pull pure positive life force energy from behind the person and into the person.

Envisioning this energy filling every single molecule of their body.

You are going to start pulling on the energy, bring it completely through the person, through the space between the two of you, and through you.

You are going to continue to pull--- pull--- pull--- the pure positive life force energy coming from behind the person, through the person, through the space in between, into you and all the way through you.

Remember, you are not keeping this energy in any way, shape or form. You are just receiving it and allowing it to go all the way through you.

You are receiving from this person in totality.

From here you are going to continue to pull and receive and allow it to go through. Pulling, receiving, being the space of allowance.

Melting the barriers, shifting and changing.

Breathing. Being present. Receiving.

The more you practice this the easier it becomes and the more you will perceive a shift in the energy. You are going to continue to pull until a lightness comes over you or your body feels completely relaxed.

From here you are going to send energy from the armpit area of your body to the person in front of you. This sending energy is going to be the energy of gratitude. Gratitude for being who they were. Gratitude for playing a part in your life. This gratitude is going from the sides of you into the sides of them through them and back into you.

The side of you is forming a circle of gratitude energy into them. Pulling still through the middle, sending back on the sides, gratitude, yummy expansion energy.

Receiving.

Sit with that temporarily. Pulling, pushing, receiving.

Know that just the intention of this happening is creating the space of this possibility. Even if you cannot envision it, just the mere act of speaking it out loud, is creating it.

You are intending this whole practice of pulling and sending and receiving. You are being the space of something different.

Now, take a moment to think about this person as they are now.

How do you feel about them?

Can you perceive the difference of space here?

What we actually did was we pulled the energy of upset from them. Now here is the deal, they can still choose upset, they still have a choice. Energetically you pulled the energy of the situation they were stuck in, whatever that was, and you actually received all the emotions attached to that. You received them until they were neutral. If you still are aware of some energy existing between the person you pulled from, do it again a few times. You want to receive them completely and their viewpoints about the situation at hand. The key here is just to receive the energy.
Allowance. You don't have to agree with what they are choosing, you just have to receive.

What you should be noticing is the situation "feels" different. Common feelings with this are:
- feeling less emotionally charged about the situation.
- feeling more relaxed about the person.
- feeling neutral to the person.
- feeling free from the situation.

I encourage you to do this exercise with everyone you ha any upset with and or anyone you feel like you upset. This will change the way you feel about others and it will change the way people feel about you.

Do this exercise with strangers who look sad in the grocery store. Do this with anyone and everyone. Get used to pulling energy from people and receiving them in totality. You will find that you can change someone's day by receiving from them. You will transform your relationships by receiving from them. You will open up your world by receiving from everyone around you, creating allowance and communion everywhere you go.

Connection Points to You

rocess helps you remove the stored energy ave to you and about you. We are going to go clearing process as we have to go into all the paces you have stored about you that are no longer serving you. This process is most successful if you are willing to be in a different space about your past.

We are going to dive first into the places that are continuously coming up for you that you do not want to look at. You know those places that are continuously there. Like maybe when your dad said you were ugly and every time you look in the mirror you are reminded of that thought, so you just stop looking in the mirror? Or maybe that time that you did something that 8-year-old you perceived as the worst thing in the whole world and you are continuously plagued with the remembrance of that time.

For me, I see this in clients all the time. These are the trigger things that keep you connected to a you, that is not really you. These things keep you small and disconnected from a life that works for you.

This process may be a hard process initially.

Often you have blocked much of the memory out and you only play the painful part of it over and over, not completing the story. This often stores the memory as not completely true. And you identify with the wrongness within the story, instead of the truth of the story as it really is.

You may have decided you are so bad and so wrong that you start looping in the wrongness instead of seeing what is real and true about the situation.

Most of the main core stuff, in the beginning, is from childhood. You have stored wrongness so deep, and what you have defined as so true, that you build the foundation of what you can and can't choose as you age, on these very core experiences.

As you use the process moving forward, please know that as you untangle the wrongness from the core, you will find other situations that match the core foundation you have been validating within the wrongness.

Your life is built on these very experiences, so when you change the energies held within them, you start to change the very way your life is showing up.

This exercise should be integrated as something you do daily for yourself for a while.

The more you do this the more aware you will become of what you are thinking about yourself.

The more you practice this the better you will get at identifying where you are sticking yourself and where you are creating situations that may or may not work for your life any longer.

The more you do this the greater expansion of you will become available.

EXERCISE

Start in a safe place. Allow your body to be in a relaxed position, especially as you read the following. Connect with your breath and expand out.

Bring forward a memory you continuously play. Pay attention to that memory for a moment.

What are you not seeing here? Receive. Expand out bigger and faster.

Where is everywhere you are making you wrong instead of seeing what's true? Untangle and unwind that. Keep your barriers down and breathe.

Make all the connection points to all of it.

Complete the story, no matter how hard.

Remind yourself you are safe.

Now cognitively you may or may not be actually mentally going there currently. It's more about going through the steps to untangle this first. Being open and vulnerable with you, to serve you and your expansion.

Breathe, stay expanded, and be with the energies you are aware of. You are safe and present. You can do this. No one has any power over you through this process.

Now go to you in this memory.

Put you out in front of you.

Pull pure positive life force energy through the you in front of you, encompassing every molecule of your little body.

Pull through you into the space in between you and into you as you are now. Receiving every single molecule of everything you were, no matter how painful it was, pulling, receiving being present with the space of you, breathing and expanding and receiving.
Now begin from the armpit area of you now and turn the energy around and send it back to the younger you receiving it in the back of you going through and back to you. Creating a circle on either side of both of your bodies. Place gratitude

energy in this circle. Sending gratitude to smaller you for choosing this journey.
Gratitude for enduring the spaces and places littler you went. Receiving the space of gratitude back inside of you. Being grateful for who you are and why you are here. Being present with you in a way you have never been before. Being the space of gratitude and allowance for who you are and what you have done.

Repeat this process for every painful memory you have in your childhood. Take them one at a time.

No need to feel overwhelmed with it.

You can choose to do one nightly.

What's amazing about this process is that when you start doing this many of the memories will fade without even clearing them. As some memories piggyback off of each other, they will fade with no clearing. You will find layers of memories to clear. Some you may not even remember. Stay present with each day and clear the ones you think about daily.

And remember

This is your universe, you get to decide.

Letting you off the hook

Today is the day you decide that you are going to stop punishing you! Seriously. Nothing you did was inexcusable. Nothing you are doing is because you are a bad person.

You are not bad. You are not wrong. You are an infinite being with infinite choice.

You have been programmed to respond in a certain way.

You have spent lifetime after lifetime in certain constructs.

You have learned the "right way" to respond.

You are mimicking other people's stuff.

You are doing what this reality told you to do.

You make mistakes.

You choose things or have chosen things in the past that maybe weren't your best choice.

And all that's okay!

Your mind is a garden, your thoughts are the seeds.

The faster you get out of making you wrong, the faster you will flow in a life that works for you.

Much of what you do or have done in the past has very little to do with you. You are and always have been aware. This idea that we came here to be or do everything relates so fully in this present moment. You came here to learn and grow, correct?

Let's say there is this boy named Tommy. Tommy was born to Sylvia and Chris. Tommy's main lesson this lifetime is to learn to trust himself. As part of his growth, he must be betrayed by others to complete his lesson, so his parents start this journey.

Chris leaves the family before Tommy is one years old. He cannot bear the burden of being a parent. Chris cannot handle the pressures of being a dad and continuously feels like a failure, but he doesn't know why.

Tommy came to this life to learn how to trust himself, in order to trust himself he must learn to not trust others. This is his unique lesson. The seeds are now existing.

Chris is aware he has to leave his son but he doesn't understand it. The urge is so strong. He internalizes the struggle, makes it his own. He says he feels like he needs to leave but doesn't know why. Everyone he talks to, tells him how wrong he is for wanting to leave. It gets stronger and stronger as he is aware that his newborn baby is telling him to leave but he has no idea how to even verbalize this? It's all energy he is receiving into his body.

Chris leaves, internalizing the struggle that there is something wrong with him, he must just be a bad guy. He never speaks to anyone about leaving his baby or the mom. He pretends it never happened as the burden of it all is too hard to bear. In all actuality he was just aware of the constructs his son was in when he was born.

His mom Sylvia, becomes the single mom. She aligns with the idea that she has to struggle because that's what single moms do right? You're not allowed to be a single mom and not struggle are you? She raises Tommy as she struggles. She works a lot as she is trying to create a different life for them. In turn she promises Tommy things she would like to provide but can't. She feels terrible about it and Tommy learns he can't trust his mom.

Now Tommy has a large section of his garden planted with the idea that he can't trust people.

You meet Tommy in his late teens. You too are a teenager. You like Tommy so much. He is so cute and kind. You just want to make Tommy happy.

Tommy has a lot of stored energy, "I can't trust people." Over half of his energy screams, "I can't trust people". You hear that energy subconsciously. You desire so badly to make Tommy happy.

You energetically align with Tommy and look to see what he desires. It's all energy. No rights or wrongs, just space.

"I am going to make Tommy really happy, so if making Tommy happy means he doesn't want to trust me then that's what I will do. I will make sure Tommy can't trust me." This is all subconscious noise. You are not aware of what you are aware of.

Then all the sudden you find yourself in weird situations acting in ways you do not like, but its like you can't help it. You are acting like an out of control a**hole and you hate it but you can't stop it. Every time you're around Tommy mean things come out of your mouth. You find yourself in a situation where you have kissed another man, you cheated on Tommy. You feel terrible. You must be the worst person on the planet. How could you do this?

You actually validated Tommy's reality. You became the effect of someone else's energy because you are aware of what people require and desire. You are aware. You are not bad or wrong.

Do you understand how that works?

You are aware of what people desire and require.

You always have been.

You are an empath who came here to fulfill certain constructs, fulfill certain roles and do things for your own expansion.

The cycle is ending.

You can be free now.

Stop punishing you for your path and choose to move forward in awareness.

You are not bad.

You are not wrong.

You are aware.

This is your universe, now you get to decide.

Get out of conclusion and feel the words you are speaking

The fastest way to get into your body awareness is to stop concluding that you already know the answer. You may hear me say this over and over in your head, in fact, I would love it if you would allow yourself to set this as an energetic marker.

Often times I will talk to people and our conversation will go as follows:

Client: "I am feeling so crappy. This happened and I feel like it happened because .... and I know it's confirmation that I am .... because I did this to this person and I am just feeling awful about it. What do I do?"

Me: And then I sit there like..... "umm ok? Did you ask any questions about that at all?"

Client: "Well no, because I know that this means this and that means that and I just don't know."

Ok, rule number one, you don't know because you have decided you know! But what you decided you know makes you feel like crap, because a lie makes you feel heavy so then you "try" and make it make sense by looping in figuring it out because you're sure if you just think about it long and hard enough the truth will magically appear, because it always does right? NOT!

Obsessing and figuring everything out has been working so well for you that I'm surprised you don't have everything all figured out by now because if you could figure it out that way don't you think you would have by now?

When you feel crappy and heavy that is the universe telling you that you are not on the right track.

Lies create heaviness. ALWAYS!

Let's take an example I recently had with a client. My client tells me that she is "terrible." She was supposed to follow through with some stuff and she didn't. She chose not to do what she was supposed to do and now she is at risk of losing a free work benefit that she has. She's feeling like she messed up. She's a loser. She never follows through with anything. She is feeling like she is a problem child, which brings her to being small and how wrong she always felt as a child.

Me: "Let's back up. Did you ask if the "free support" is helping you? Or something else?"

Client: "No I never asked. I "assumed" because it was free it was contributing to my life."

Me: "Is it? Is it contributing to your life? Or something else? Is it creating chaos? or something else?

Client: "Oh, I never even considered it wasn't contributing."

Me: "Are you capable of having the life that you want if you continue to keep this benefit? So what if what has you feeling heavy is the lie that you even require this?"

And right there she has space again. She has a lightness in her body. The heaviness fades away and she giggles over the phone.

Client: "Wow. What if I'm really not as bad as I think I am?"

I know it's easy to relate to your past and create a scenario to play in.

Today is the day you become aware of the words you are saying.

Feel them in your body.

When you speak does it make you feel lighter or does it make you feel like a ton of lead is on top of you?

The truth will always set you free. Always.

Just because you hear it in your head doe not make it true

Your head comes up with lots of crap. You have been taught to obsess and worry about everything. Often times people confuse the head noise for awareness and I am going to tell you right now that probably at least 80 percent of what you hear, if not more, is not true. It's scenarios your head is looping in.

When you hear your head say,
"Why did you do that? Your such a bad mom."

Don't align with it like, "OMG, I am a bad mom. I'm such a bad mom. Why am I always a bad mom."

No. Stop and ask.

"Truth am I a bad mom? Or something else?" Breathe.

Then say. "Ok well, I am not a bad mom. I am a good mom. My children love and respect me. I am doing a great job at this mom thing. I am an awesome mom and I am proud of who I am."

Plant that. Stand in that. Know that you can create anything and if being an awesome mom is on the list of what you want to create then choose it.

Your head is going to come up with some freaky stupid stuff.

If what your head is telling you makes you feel:
- panicky, it's not true.
- yucky, it's not true.
- heavy, it's not true.
- bad about yourself, it's not true.

, your truth always expands.

you are in your head and you are looping in this
you're a bad mom and someone's going to take your
kids away. Does that thought create a lightness? Or a heaviness?

If you are in your head looping in this idea that you are going to go broke because you aren't going to have enough money to pay your house payment in 6 months. Does that thought make you feel lighter or heavier?

Just because you hear it in your head, does not make it true. True awareness you feel in your body. It expands you. It creates a lightness. It makes you feel like you are moving in the right direction, even if the right direction for you is claiming bankruptcy and letting your house go. That may actually be lighter for you than keeping your house and making payments!

So ask questions about what's coming up for you in your head.

Ask first "Is it _____" or something else. Get in the habit of breaking down the questions.

Whatever you heard your head say-- followed by or something else.

Feel what feels lighter.

From there if something else feels lighter go to the ask and receive.

- What would it take to get the information I require?
- What would it take for this to be ease?
- What else is possible here that I have never considered?

Receive this information into your heart space and stay out of your head! Just be.

This is a process of learning how to be different. As you collect information you will receive more and more information until you have collected enough to have a cognitive "awareness."
The awareness will be light and will create space in your body. If you're still looping, you more than likely have not gotten to the awareness yet. There are two different choices that will affect how fast you will move on an awareness.

If you are looking at a small choice, like what would my body like to eat? Or what do I do about my neighbor's dogs barking, you may ask a few questions and get the awareness instantly.

If you're looking at a big choice, like when should I leave my husband or what do I do about my boyfriend's drug problem? You are going to want to sit on that and ask and receive a lot.

You want to make a choice from expansion not from head noise.

You want to make a choice that is light and sets you free. Choosing to leave your husband tomorrow because you got the awareness of it today may not be your best choice. But sitting and receiving information like, "What would it take for this to be ease? What can me and my body be to create this situation as ease?" Asking and receiving will create an opening of time and space that will allow a shift to happen without upset. It will create you having the information you require to change the marriage, creating as much ease as possible for everyone involved. That may or may not look like divorce. It will allow things to shift and change and show up that facilitate change with more ease.

Breathing and being present with what shows up. Make your decisions based on how they feel. This will create you showing up and having more ease in your body and your life. Your head does not know how to cognitively create ease, but your body and the universe do. The universe has a million possibilities for you, your head only has the freak out from the past. It's time to choose the unknown. It's time to choose the ease.

Everything has a reason

Everything is showing up in your life for a reason.

Nothing is by mistake.

You created a life road map long before you embodied.

You decided to play in a big story here.

This is what has been created for you to exist lifetime after lifetime.

You have karmic debt.

You have created an energetic road map to remember the promises you have made.

You have things your soul agreed to. And the pacts that you have made.

This goes so far and so deep. Nothing is random.

The key to ease is to not make anything that shows up wrong and not project wrongness from your past to your future.

Allow yourself to be present in the moment always.

No blaming and shaming yourself, or others, for anything that is currently showing up is key.

It's all just an experience.

If it is an experience you don't like, then you and only you have the power to change that.

You are the creator and the master of your universe.

You have the power to change and rearrange anything.

Feel the power in that.

There was a time you were powerless, yes. But the world has changed.

The frequencies have now aligned in your personal power area.

You now have the space and the ability to create something different in your life.

All it takes is some present intention and thought.

You truly can create anything you desire.

Anything is within your capacity to create.

In fact, even reading these very words has a reason!

Understanding that everything you have experienced has brought you to this very moment. Every awareness about something you would like to create is entirely possible.

Nothing you have ever thought is outside of your realm of creation. You just have to put enough focus attention on it, imprint it into your space for long enough, and bam. Before you know it you are smack dab in the middle of a new amazing creation.

Every path has its lessons. Every encounter up to this point has had meaning. Now it's in your court. You have the power to change anything and create anything you desire!

What would you like to create with the information you already have?

What if you used all those past experiences to propel you forward and create beyond anything you ever imagined?

You are an empathic person with skills and capacities that are unmatched.

What are you going to choose to do now?

It's your universe. You get to decide.

Projections and Expectations

Projections and Expectations are energetic markers that have more to do with outsiders upholding energies than within yourself. Every one of us upholds projections and expectations for others.

Projections

Projections are automatic responses based on your belief system that you project on others about what they can and cannot have, do or be.

So let's take a common projection, a 13 year old child. You have automatic projections, based on your decisions and belief systems that you assume are true for a 13 year old. All the things they should be doing or not doing. These projections have an autoresponder that creates equal and opposite energy within the person.

If you have a random encounter with a 13 year old who is doing something outside of what you have decided is acceptable for a 13 year old, you will automatically project at them.

Let's say you see a 13 year old at the mall shopping during the day by themselves. You may think, "OMG! Why is that child not in school. They should be at school, they must be skipping. They are a bad person."

You will energetically project your point of view at the teenager. The teenager will feel your projection and either they will resist and react (get stuck in anger) or agree and align (I am a terrible person. I should be like everyone else.)

If the teenager resists and reacts, they will become in resistance of the energy creating an uneasy, unidentifiable wrongness. If the teenager aligns and agrees with your projection they solidify your viewpoint as the "right" thing.

What is important to understand about projections is, they are autoresponders. They are automatic based on your viewpoints. So if you wanted to change that, as we have talked about before, you must reduce your points of views about who or what anyone is choosing, doing or being.

Have you ever been around someone who has a strong viewpoint about how you should be living your life? It's uncomfortable and not pleasant. If you have family members who have strong viewpoints about how you should live, their projections are causing an inner battle of self-worth within your system. The projections of who you should be and how you should live are hard to get out from underneath.

Let's take another example, an addict who has gone to jail, who would like to get out and be clean. This is a very hard one to shift, especially if he stole from family members. No one will want to house him after he gets out because they will be in a constant projection that he will steal again, he will use again. That's why the percentage of people who have been to jail and go back is so high. Energetically it's very hard to out create that situation. People are projecting at them everything they used to be and their own fear of them creating it again, instead of creating a place free to choose.

Which ties into expectations.

Expectations

Expectations are where you project what you expect of other people. In expectation, there is no choice, no possibility, no freedom. When you are stuck in expectations of others you are literally shrinking their life and your life and the life that is available to both of you. If you want to truly be free in this reality you have to free yourself from expecting anything from anyone.

Expectations are a killer of possibility by your decision points to what "should" be created. Expectations create an energetic resistance and reaction because within expectation is the ability to disappoint and upset others.

If you truly want to be free you have to get that everyone in this reality is here to walk their own path and their own truth. When you allow those around you, those you love to truly embrace their path and make their own decisions, without your projections or expectations, you truly allow them to live.

I had an instance in my awakening where a family member was continuously telling me how my decisions about my life disappointed and upset her. I get that she was letting me know how she felt but the reality is it wasn't decisions about her life, they were about mine and how I choose to live my life. The decisions she was upset with were how I spent my money and how I raised my children. Literally nothing to do with her. She insisted on continuing to let me know every time I was with her about how I choose to live my life was making her upset.

So I let her know, she could either get over it or she could not see me anymore. The projection and expectations at me on decisions that did not directly affect her life had nothing to do with her. She was trying to control and dominate my decisions based on her own point of view about what she could have not me. And that did not work for me.

What she was actually caught in was the hatred she had in her own life about how she felt like she wasn't able to choose what she wanted to. Instead of seeing what I was doing and using it to propel her life forward she had to continuously make me wrong.

She randomly projected at me that I couldn't afford things. Saying things like, that's too expensive, you shouldn't buy that, it's unnecessary. That's outrageous, I can't believe you're going to pay that much money for that. Well?? It's my money and I get to decide how I want to spend it. I didn't owe her anything. I also didn't depend on her for money.

For most of my life, I aligned and agreed with those ideas. I stayed small in the shell of making sure everyone agreed with what I was choosing until I became me.

Until I cleared spaces and places of me and realized I can have anything I desire. It's not about money or how much something costs, it's about the value it adds to your life.

I explained that to her. That the value of what this product was going to add to my life was enough for me to choose to buy it and her projecting at me that I couldn't have it didn't work for me.

She continued on. I could see that her projections again had nothing to do with me and everything to do with her ability to choose something greater. Again I made it known that it wasn't going to work for me and my family.

It's been years since we spoke and my life and my wealth has grown exponentially since deciding not to allow that in my life.
Which brings us to the final section in this chapter......

When expectations create separations

When you function in a space of continuous expectation of someone you create a separation of them and an emptiness in you. What you expect of someone else has very little to do with them and everything to do with you. When you continuously expect, you are telling them energetically and potentially verbally that their choices aren't good enough for you. What that creates is a continuous cycle of wrongness.

What you want to do is look at the behavior someone is exhibiting.

Is it directly harmful to you? More than likely not.

It may have hurt your feelings but that's yours, not theirs. You have to learn to meet people where they are, not where you want them to be.

If someone is exhibiting behavior that is not directly harmful to you, you have to ask yourself why do you care? Making them wrong for the behavior is not going to change it. If they are exhibiting a behavior around you that makes you feel a certain way, you have choices. You can, let them know that the behavior they are exhibiting does not work for you. The way it makes you feel, does not work for you.

Do not make them wrong.

Let them do or be whatever it is they are doing and being but let them know that if it continues this will be your plan of action.

Set your boundaries. Let them know that this behavior creates this feeling for you and you don't desire to feel this way.

Then give them space.

Do not make them wrong for choosing it.

If they would like to change the behavior talk to them about other ways to deal with it.

If they like the behavior and don't see anything wrong with it, then move on.

And most importantly don't resist or react to the behavior.

Every time you resist and react you are creating a projection and an expectation which further solidifies the upset and the behavior.

Breathe. Do some energy pulls. Stand in what works for you and be in allowance of what they are creating.

Often I work with people who are in relationships. They continuously tell me how upset they are with their spouses' behavior. And I explain, you have to stop being upset, upset creates more upset!

In this life, there is what works for you and what doesn't.

Start demanding what does work for you to show up and stop entertaining the crazy train. When someone expects you to do something and you don't, does it make you feel good about yourself or bad? Stop projecting wrongness and realize the issues have to be cleared up both ways.

Expectations of those around you create separation in your relationship. If that's what you're trying to create then great, create that. But if not, you have to find a different way to respond.

Expectations create separations.

Is the behavior directly harmful to them?

If so reread above and realize making them wrong is not going to fix the toxic behavior and they may even be creating it because of the projections of wrongness. Want them to show up differently? Give them space to be different. Give them allowance to be what they desire to be. And support them in whatever they choose.

If this feels too hard to do for someone, or someone to do for you, then let them go and find someone who will do that for them or for you, because everyone in this world deserves to feel supported and loved.

What if nothing anyone chooses is ever wrong?

Chapter Four
Untangling the lies of this reality

Lies or information that is not true

If you are stuck in the energy of a lie or something that is not true, you can never change it. It creates a heavy tangle for your body and your being.

This is also true for large paradigms in this reality. Many systems, let's take religion, have parts and pieces that are true, but much of it has been manipulated by viewpoints. Much of the information we read, see on the news, interact with daily, is only part true. When you identify or believe in a system that is only part true it starts to create a heaviness, anxiety or upset in your world.

Have you ever been part of something and then one day realize you just don't want to do it anymore? You may not have an explanation as to why, it just feels yucky. More than likely you were aware that something about it just doesn't work for you anymore. Within that system there was probably a lie that you were aware of.

If you grew up believing something that isn't actually true, you are aware on some level it isn't true, right? Like you know it's not and you try hard to believe it. But in reality, you were aware it wasn't true. And then one day someone says something or does something and the truth comes out. And all the sudden you're like, wait a minute? And everything makes sense. And this lightness comes over your body and your life and you knew it! You knew it was a lie! And all the sudden you have freedom.

It's the same with any other situation. When something isn't true it feels weird for you. It feels tangled, heavy, and hard like you're trying to move forward but every direction you go is not letting you in. You have to untangle yourself from the viewpoint.

There is freedom in releasing the lies.

There is also some sort of value in not knowing the truth. There is fear in the truth. What if you find out something awful about yourself right? Everything all of that is, can you choose to remove all of it from all of your universes and can you choose that now? Vaporize it out. You will not discover anything awful about you or your life.

What you will discover in this chapter will give your body a sense of lightness and freedom. Let's release yourself from the lies of this reality and give yourself space to follow your truth.

Forgiveness

Forgiveness is not something that actually helps to "heal" any situation or give you peace. Forgiveness creates a void energy that says I choose to be the bigger person and forgive you. If you want to truly be free from someone, pull energy, bring forward all the emotions between you, receive them all, and send back gratitude. The charge should be removed. Once the charge is removed, clear out your viewpoints about what they did that was bad or wrong. Give them space to show up as the person they are. Acknowledge their role and yours. No one does anything to you without your permission.

When you "forgive" someone you still hold the energetic markers for what they did.

You still uphold the projections of it and you still hold the space of it. You don't want to forgive people. You want to clear it and acknowledge what you know about the situation. When you clear it, you no longer have to be held hostage to it. You no longer have to uphold any of it and you release yourself from the obligations of it. When you forgive you still have those things.

Just because you remove the charge does not mean that you still have to choose to have the person in your life anymore. If someone doesn't work for you, clear the crap and then set them free. More times than not if they don't work for you, you don't work for them and you're both holding each other back. Use your energy wisely and create a space for you to show up fully in your life.

Trust

Trust is a fancy way to project unawareness, unconsciousness, and expectations on others. When you say I trust you or I trust that ... you are basically saying you're not willing to be aware.

I recently had someone message me saying that she trusted that one of my programs was going to "make her less scattered." When I looked at that, I was aware she didn't ask any questions. She was looking for something to help her become less scattered. Instead of actively searching for something that would create her being less scattered, she just randomly choose something and then projected her "trust" at it. And the thing is, no where did it say this program was going to help anyone become more organized or less scattered. It was like she just choose it and decided what it was going to create. This is one way people keep perpetuating a cycle of unawareness, we all have been guilty of it at some point in our life. Now, when my program that she projected at doesn't make her less scattered, even though nowhere does it claim that, she can blame me and my products instead of taking responsibility for herself.

It's like when people give a teenager a car and then they do something reckless with it.

They say, "I trusted that they would be responsible. And they let me down."

Well did you ask if they would be responsible? Or did you just decide they would? Cause there's a HUGE difference.

When someone is unfaithful in a marriage and people say I trusted them with my heart and they broke it. Did you check in and see if that person wanted your heart? Did you ask if they were able to care for your heart? Do they even desire to be in relationship with you? Are you actively asking questions about your relationship? Or did you just decide to "trust" them 15 years ago and then never look at it again? Bingo.

People decide and live their lives from past decisions and decide everything will stay the same.

This world is always changing.

Nothing stays the same forever. And why would you want it to? Trust is not somewhere you want to function. Trust literally takes out the question. It puts you into a place of unawareness and allows you to function in unconsciousness.

Definition of trust
Acceptance of the truth of a statement without evidence or investigation.
Another definition
The state of being responsible for someone or something.

If you want someone to be responsible for something of yours whether it's your heart or your car, you may want to ask if they are capable of caring for it without assuming so. Stop using trust to take you out of being aware.

There is something wrong with you

You may have grown up with someone always asking you, "What's wrong with you?"

Every belly ache, every pain, "there must be something wrong with you?"

What if nothing is wrong with you ever?

What is the lie is, "there is something wrong with you?"

Feeling overwhelmed?

Feeling unsettled?

Over emotional?

Highly agitated?

Whose upset is that? Is it yours? Someone else's? Or something else's?

What if what you are experiencing doesn't even belong to you?

When you read that, does it make you feel heavier? Or lighter?

Is it possible what you are "feeling" is a collective amount of energy, space and consciousness? And none of it is a wrongness of you?

Think about the feeling you have been identifying with, you have been feeling ......(sad).

Do you actually have a reason to feel ....(sad)?
Is it possible everything you have been feeling is just energy you have been perceiving? After all your body is a receiving organ, receiving information from everyone all the time.

What if there is nothing "wrong" with you ever?

What if everything you have been identifying with is just an awareness of a frequency nearby?

Take a deep breath. You feel the difference now?

Is now the time to stop identifying with emotions that aren't yours?

Make sure you are staying in your awareness about what is yours and what isn't.

You are an aware person receiving information from everyone all the time.

Take a deep breath.

You do not have to take it all on.

It's okay to release everything that isn't yours.

There is nothing wrong with you. Ever.

You have to figure everything out

This. You do not have to figure everything out. You are not the knower of all things. The universe has a million possibilities for every situation. And here you are with two answers, none of which you like, trying to figure out what to choose.

Stop looping over and over trying to figure stuff out. Looping takes you out of being present and puts you back into your reference points to the past. There is nothing new for you there. I know it's hard at first. We are so programmed to go right back to the space of figuring it out with our heads. Your head does not know any new information. Your head is only going to show you what you already know.

If you want to go beyond the issue or have choices that work for you, stop trying to figure it out. You have to stop listening to the words, "You have to get this right."

Everything is changeable.

Nothing is concrete.

A choice is only as good as long as you make it. Stop buying into the lie that once you make a choice you have to choose it forever. You can choose one thing today and choose something different tomorrow. Nothing is concrete.

Here are common reasons why you're looping.

You have already decided what is going to happen in the future and now you're doing damage control.

Ex. I won't have enough money to pay my bills this month. You are freaking out trying to figure out what your going to do when you don't pay your bills.

Okay. So you "decided" you can't pay your bills. Great. Did you ask any questions? If this is one of your worries, I'm going to go out on a limb here and say this is a common worry for you, which is why you always have this problem. Do not project your past at your future. Breathe, expand out and ask some questions. What can you receive to create this as ease? What would it take to have money show up right away? Stop deciding that you can't create in your future. You are not there yet.

You have way too much polarity around it, too much right and wrong, good and bad. Ex. You want to quit your job, but you're scared you're never going to find one that pays you the same or has the same benefits or has nice people or whatever you are trying to solidify. Take a deep breath, expand out, clear all the polarity. "Where is everywhere you decided you're never going to find a job you love?" Vaporize, vaporize, vaporize.

Ask some questions. "What can I receive to have a job I love with ease?" You do not have to know the answer. Allow the universe to give you some new possibilities. Get clear about what you do want and ask for it.

You have major anxiety about making a choice about something.

Somewhere you're stuck in a lie around it. Ex. If I choose to do ....., then either this will happen that will be good or this will happen that will be bad.
Look at the anxiety you are having. Write down all the possible outcomes and then clear the crap out of them. Realize everything you came up with is only one possibility. And it's not even one you have to create. Remind yourself

that you are a powerful creator. This is your universe, you get to decide.

You're focusing on the problem instead of a possibility or an easy solution. Ex. Someone is going to be mad at me because I did something I said I wasn't going to. Expand out. Breathe. Pull energy through whatever you feel is unchangeable. Change the energy around it and then implant the energy of something different showing up. It takes two people to align to one idea to make it real and true. What if you stopped believing?

You do not have to figure everything out. You have a toolbox of magical solutions. Use them.

You have to have a reason to say no

This reality wants you to always have a reason and justification for everything.

You aren't allowed to just say no.

Well today is the day you change that.

Today is the day you start standing in honoring you.

If it doesn't feel light and expansive don't choose it.

Today I give you permission to say no to anything that just feels yucky.

No more resistance.

No more making you wrong for not choosing something everyone else thinks you should.

When you start making choices for yourself and really truly standing in those choices it's not as scary as you think. Somewhere in your brain, you have concocted this whole scenario of what is going to happen if you go against what other people think you should choose. You have held them at a higher standard than you hold yourself. You have given them more permission than you have given yourself.

Right now let's take your power back. Clear your space of other people's opinion. Create a space for you to have what you desire. Now is the time for you to stand in what works for you!

Emotional upset is normal

There is nothing fun or expansive about being overly emotional. Functioning in emotional upset takes you out of being present in your life. It continues to plant more emotional upset in your field. It also attracts more things to be emotional about.

When you function in emotional upset it tangles you in an emotional distractor pattern. This pattern completely takes you out of having any choice on how you react.

Have you ever been so mad you had no control over what you did or what you said?

Have you been caught in a stage of emotional sadness and grief that lasted for years that you couldn't stop?

There are many main emotional distractor systems. Each system includes energies that keep you looping and ping pong off each other creating an energy that makes them hard to release. The systems include:

Anger and rage- These keep you from choosing beyond your current circumstances and keep you looping in upset.

Blame and shame- These keep you from being the creator of your reality. They loop you into a system of unawareness about your life and how your choices create.

Regret and guilt- These keep you looping in your past. Giving you no space to create something different.

Compulsive and obsessive thoughts- These keep you from what you know to be true. They distract you from your own truth. These mostly stop you from seeing the lies others projected at you.

Love and jealousy- These keep you in projections and expectations. They stop you from functioning in awareness of the present moment and keep you looping in an old choice. Once you choose to love someone you cannot see what they are choosing themselves.

Fear and doubt- These keep you from choosing to expand your life, hiding yourself from commitment.

When you clear the distractors completely you get to have a different choice in your life.

Next is a series of clearings to start breaking up the cycle of distractors. Please note that these clearings alone may not shift it completely. I personally have found it takes lots of consciousness and lots of presence around the cycle to clear it. I have created a program, my very first audio program that has six months of defined clearing for emotional upset. It is vigilant work and lots of choosing to clear yourself completely. If you're struggling I do suggest checking out the clearings. In this next exercise there are a series of clearings to get you started.

EXERCISE

Start first with connecting to your breath. 1-2-3. 1-2-3. Put your barriers down and expand all the way out to the space of you.

The following clearings are helpful to repeat often. You may even like to write them down and revisit them a few times a day.

If you're struggling with:
Anger and rage
- Where is everywhere I am stuck in the ping pong of upset? Vaporize.
- What is everything that keeps me tangled in the cycle of anger? Vaporize. ☐
- Where is everywhere I am addicted to being mad? Vaporize.
- What is everything I am not allowed to change? Vaporize.
- Where is everywhere I am not allowed to have space and ease? Vaporize.

Blame and shame
- What is everything that keeps me from being responsible for me? Vaporize.
- Where is everywhere someone or something has power over my choices? Vaporize.
- What is everything that creates me unaware of my actions? Vaporize.
- Where is everywhere I am not allowed to have choice in my life? Vaporize.
- What is everything that creates me in a cycle beyond my choice? Vaporize.

Regret and Guilt
- Where is everywhere I am stuck in the past? Vaporize.
- What is everything holding me to who I used to be and what I used to choose? Vaporize.
- Where is everywhere I am not allowed to change? Vaporize.
- What is everything holding me to my old pathways? Vaporize.
- Where is everywhere I am not allowed to move forward with my life? Vaporize.

Compulsive and Obsessive Thoughts
- What is everything that keeps me from seeing what's real and true? Vaporize.
- Where is everywhere I am not allowed to choose for myself? Vaporize.
- What is everything that blocks me from knowing me? Vaporize.
- Where is everywhere I am tangled in someone else's truth? Vaporize.
- What is everything that stops me from having all of me? Vaporize.

Love and Jealousy
- Where is everywhere I am not allowed to know what's true? Vaporize.
- What is everything that keeps me tangled in old choices? Vaporize.
- Where is everywhere I am not present in the moment? Vaporize.
- What are all the decisions I made that I am not allowed to choose again? Vaporize.
- Where is everywhere I am functioning in the past? Vaporize.

Fear and Doubt
- What is everything that stops me from choosing my truth? Vaporize.
- Where is everywhere I am not allowed to access what's true for me? Vaporize.
- What is everything I am not allowed to see, be, do or choose? Vaporize.
- Where is everywhere I am not allowed to know what's real and true? Vaporize.
- What is everything that creates me unwilling to move forward? Vaporize.

Be the space to look at and clear this stuff. It will change your life.

Repeat these statements:

I am an infinite being with infinite choice.

Who I was yesterday, does not define who I am today.

This is my universe, I get to decide.

I am capable of creating anything I desire.

I am the creator and the master of my reality.

I have the power to be whoever I choose to be whenever I choose to be it.

Love is the answer

You see this everywhere on social media right? Love is the answer. Well here's the problem with that. Love has a million definitions. My definition of love is different than your definition of love. Some definitions are more restricting than others, but they are all based upon certain ideas of projections and expectations.

Love is very restrictive and doesn't hold much space for change. It's very definable. And if someone says they "loved" you it comes with certain expectations of how to love them back and what's required of you based on the action. Love holds many source points for many people. Most people have loved and lost. Most people have had their heart broken. If you have experienced a hard break up. Your definition of love encompasses that. So if you project your definition of love on someone else it holds that vibration of upset.

Gratitude

Gratitude is the space we are truly looking for. Gratitude has an expansive energy that does not come with definition or expectation. Gratitude expands whatever it comes in contact with. Gratitude creates more space and more possibility. Spread gratitude in this world.

Just feel this in your body:
"I choose to have love for this world."
"I choose to have gratitude for this world."
Which one feels more expansive? Breathe and ask again.
"I choose to have love for this world."
"I choose to have gratitude for this world."
Take a deep breath. Share the one that creates the most.

Life is a struggle

I hear people say this all the time! "The struggle is real!" Do you have any idea what you are telling the universe when you say that over and over? You are basically planting struggle all over the place! Do you like struggle? Is struggle valuable to you? Do you enjoy struggle?

Much of the awareness process is really becoming aware of what you are telling the universe. If you are done struggling, stop continually projecting it. Come to the understanding that everything you are experiencing is a direct result of what's planted.

Understand it takes some time and space to change it, but it's totally changeable. The faster you stop joking and creating struggle as some fun carnival game the quicker your life will change.

Your life is only a struggle because you have decided it is. You are a powerful creator. Time to make a different choice!

Clear it out:
- "Where is everywhere I have decided my life is a struggle?" Vaporize.
- "What is everything I have agreed to struggle about?" Vaporize.
- "Where is everywhere I am addicted to struggle?" Vaporize.
- "What is everything upholding struggle in my life?" Vaporize.

Release struggle and choose something else!

Perpetrating the wrongness

As I was making my transition through consciousness and awareness I was really choosing to start doing what worked for me. As a single mom, feeling stressed out and overwhelmed one of the things I really hated about my life was the way I reacted in anger.

As my journey progressed I understood that I was in charge of the way I wanted my life to feel. If something was not working for me, I stopped choosing it. If something was creating a certain feeling in my life that I didn't like, I stopped choosing it. I learned I could have the space to choose what works for me and what doesn't.

I would talk often to my kids about this, often saying things like,

"Yes I know that's how I have done things in the past, but that doesn't actually work for me."

Or "I don't like the way I responded there so let me try that again."

Or "I actually don't want to be that person anymore so let me start over."

What that started to create is a whole new dialog in my home. My children were young at the time, my youngest daughter was like six. I wanted her to know that the angry mom I was in the past was not going to continue to carry over.

One day I took them all to go blueberry picking. My youngest daughter had a real issue with being angry as well, go figure! One of the things she did daily was, she would say she wanted to do something or eat something or choose something and when it would come time to do it, eat or go there, she would decide she didn't want to do it anymore.

Like every single day. This frustrated me so bad. To get three kids ready to go somewhere or do something and then have one of them say, "no I don't want to anymore," and then refuse to participate. It boiled my blood. My normal reaction was always to freak out. Yell, scream and lose my sh*t. Then I would force her to participate. It was never enjoyable. And often she would cause such a scene we would end up leaving anyway.

We had just arrived at the blueberry fields. We drove there, went in the store, bought containers to fill with blueberries then drove to the field. We piled out of the car and my youngest daughter says, "I don't want to pick blueberries anymore." I'm like you have got to be kidding me? I didn't actually say that though, but what I did is say, "ok that's fine. You can stand here. We are all going to pick blueberries. Come on girls let's go." And there she stood.

This tiny little peanut who weighed like 38 pounds with her arms crossed and her mad face. I made a choice and I was not engaging in that crazy, so I didn't. I left her right there with her arms all crossed in anger and I went and picked blueberries. I stayed close enough by that I could see her and I watched as she stood in surprise. I wasn't arguing with her. I wasn't yelling or screaming. She was so surprised I just left her. As her arms faded from the crossed position and her body started melting into a more comfortable position.

I walked over to her and said, "You ready to pick some blueberries? Come on they are so yummy!"
And I kind of forced one in her little mouth. "No" she snapped back.

And I said "ok, well will you take a walk with me? Can we look at all the yummy bushes? You don't have to pick any, just walk with me." She agreed.

As we walked I could see that she wanted to pick some, but she just couldn't allow herself to do it. And so I said, "You can pick some now, its ok."

"No I can't." she responded. "If I do you're going to make me wrong."

And I was like, "What? No I am not! Why would I do that?"

She said, "You will, you always do. You always say things like, see I told you." She continued, "If I pick blueberries and have fun doing it, when we leave you're going to say, see I told you, you would have fun."

And I thought about that statement, and she was right. I did that often. I would make her participate and then I would tell her she was wrong. As a mom that was never my intent. I definitely wasn't trying to make her wrong, but I absolutely did that often.

So I said, "I am so sorry. Mommy never wanted to make you feel wrong. If I promise and pinky swear to you that I will not say that, will you pick blueberries with me?"

And she agreed. We went on to pick blueberries for the next hour and I had the best grown up conversations with that baby girl that day. And let me tell you it really took some awareness with my words to not do that again. Once I understood how those words affected her and what that projection did to her little world, I promised myself to be aware of the wrongness I was projecting. And to stay aware of what my words where creating for others.

Autoresponders of wrongness

There is a place deep within ourselves where we are caught in a loop of auto responding in wrongness and we continue over and over perpetrating the patterns. You know that place where you say something and you can literally feel the reaction in the other person? And you think, "Why in the world did I just say that?"

Yeah that place. That place is a system you are stuck in. It's a system that keeps you locked into creating wrongness for others. It's like you don't want to choose to do that, you might even hate that you do it but you just can't seem to change it.

Let's clear it.
- Where is everywhere I am stuck perpetrating wrongness? Vaporize.
- Where is everywhere I am more dedicated to making people wrong instead of right? Vaporize.
- Where is everywhere I have to choose to make someone wrong? Vaporize.
- Where is everywhere it's easier to ignore the wrongness and continue to create it? Vaporize.
- Where is everywhere I don't have a choice? Vaporize.

The thing that really changed this for me was:
1. Allowing myself to really be aware of creating it.
2. Actively choosing to stop creating it. Like if I did it, going right to apologizing. Even if it was days before I realized I did it. I would go to the person and say, "I'm sorry I said what I said. I didn't mean it. Please forgive me. I do not want to be that kind of person anymore."

This really added some vulnerability to my life. I realized that if I wanted to have peace and ease in my life I had to stop making everyone around me wrong. I literally had to stop engaging and continuing the cycles. I started apologizing for my actions, even if it was days later. One of the things I noticed with the autoresponders is it is so ingrained that it's hard to catch.

Sometimes I didn't even realize I did it till the next day and then it felt insignificant. But it's not. It's important to do it right at that moment. Call, text, find the person and say, "I'm sorry I did what I did or said what I said. I don't want to be that person anymore and I'm really trying to change that. So if I do it again will you call me out on it? I really want to change this."

Little by little I did it. I changed the way I was responding and my choice to stop doing it. That created enough space that not only was I not choosing it, I was aware when the thoughts even entered my mind and I was able to clear them and move on. And I would like to add, this is not about over apologizing for everything. This is about apologizing when you project wrongness at someone. There's a huge difference.

It was so freeing. I am so grateful for awareness and new possibility.

Chapter Five
Getting clear about what you want to create

Choice Creates

Your choice always creates.

When you choose something, the universe starts conspiring to make it happen.

The closer you are to a choice the faster it happens, the further away from the choice you are the longer it takes.

The thing that is important about choosing things, is you really have to choose it. There's no wishing and hoping. It's like I am choosing this and I am confident it will show up. You can ask and receive to actualize more of the energy of it. But you have to stay out of the disappointment or upset that it's not happening or not happening fast enough. You also have to realize that the path to it may look different than you decided it does. When choosing things you have to choose it and get out of the conclusion about what you have to do, what has to show up and what it looks like.

There are two types of choices: Active choices and dormant choices.

An active choice is one that continues to expand and grow with you as you expand and grow. It continues to shift and change opening up new possibilities continually. When a new possibility arises make sure it matches the energy of the choice you are making. The more you ask and receive about a choice, the more you become the space of it.

A dormant choice is more of a choice you make and then leave it. Like "Man, I would really like some tacos. I wonder what it would take to have some tacos in my life?" Then you don't do anything and your neighbor shows up with tacos. These choices have a very unattached feeling to them. You make the choice and you let it go. The universe then responds.

When you make any choice it has a certain frequency to it. An active choice may have more energy required to create it. The more you receive the energy of the choice, the more of the frequency you receive. The more you really get the space of it. From there it's easy to frequency match to a choice.

Frequency matching occurs when you have a clear space "feeling" of what you are looking for. Then something shows up, feel it. Really feel it. Don't decide just because something shows up, it's a match. Stay out of the emotional attachment to it. Really look at the aspects of it.

It's common, when you're asking for things, for multiple things to show up. If you are present with what shows up, you may find it's close to what you are asking for but it may not be an exact frequency match. Stay present. Acknowledge what you are aware of. Ask and receive it to see if it matches the energy you are looking for.

Here's a process you can use to "feel" if what shows up matches what you are looking for.
Ask
"If I choose this what will my life feel like?"
"If I don't choose this what will my life feel like?"
"What will this create in my life?"

If it expands you and feels like a similar energy to what you desire, you choose the choice. Fully choose it. Even if its silently in your head.

Say, "I am choosing.........."

Really get into what that choice creates in your life. From there if the choice expands you, you continue to choose it. If it starts to contract you, you don't choose it.

An active choice has a constant uplevel

One of my active choices has been to have more money than I can spend. What this active choice has created is a constant flow of new possibilities that contribute to me financially.

When I first started choosing to have more money than I can spend, my husband was working about ninety minutes from home and he was staying all week in a hotel. So he would leave for work Monday morning and stay in a hotel for four nights and then come home for the weekend. He did this because he was working long hours and coming home just to sleep didn't make much sense. When we started asking and receiving he started getting tons of requests from work to travel. He was gone all week anyway so it didn't really matter to us if he was gone out of state. He started traveling for weeks at a time to other facilities. Because he was traveling for work, work paid for his hotel and all his food, giving us more money from his paycheck. Then he received a hefty raise to top it all off! He is now making more money than he has ever made. This active choice continues to expand giving us more and more possibilities all the time.

A dormant choice is something you make and then never or hardly revisit. This choice may still be something you receive, it just may be days or years later. It's like something you think about and put some space into it, one day it actualizes.

Years ago, I was taking lots of classes and doing coaching with a facilitator. This facilitator always had the sound of birds in the background. I always loved it so much and thought one day I too will have birds in the background. I left it. Here we are about seven years later and I have a bird who makes bird noises in the back of all my audios. I have now had her for a year and I never even realized until recently how that had materialized! It shows up often unexpectedly and reminds me that I really do get everything I ask for!

Acknowledgement is a big part of this as well. Always acknowledge when you create something. Celebrate when something shows up. Have gratitude for what you create. Every little win adds up to more space of what you want your life to be like. After a while all those little choices create BIG change!

Realizing that your choices always create, think about everything you choose today?

Where you present with each possibility?

Or did you complain and choose upset about what happened during your day?

Every single thought, emotion, feeling, it all contributes to the creation of your reality.

Really get into the habit of continuously looking at what you want to create for your life and how you want your life to show up. The more time you spend in the expansive energy of creation, inviting in what is light and fun and free. The more time you are invoking those energies into your life. The more of an invitation to the future you are becoming. The more space you are receiving to actualize the very things you desire.

We live in a frequency based universe.

This universe knows no right or wrong, no good or bad. Suffering only creates more things to suffer about. I get that it's very hard to "just stop" suffering. I am very aware that it's not that easy. That is why I have created this book. When you understand how very powerful your thoughts and actions are you can start to separate yourself from the things you no longer desire. That separation gives you more space to make better choices and allow yourself to really get what you are creating.

Every day you choose again and again. You do your best with the tools you have that day. And you try again the next day.
Keep in your awareness where you're going, and if you aren't sure, just keep going. The path will present itself. Stay in your awareness. Keep moving. Keep going. Keep choosing. Keep asking. Keep receiving. Keep where you're going in your awareness. Choosing it over and over. Know one day you're landing where you're supposed to go. And from there, just keep choosing.
Choose more and more, every day choose more. Know that some days you may not make the best choice and that's okay, keep going. Keep choosing, keep moving, keep going. Don't stop because you made a mistake!

Acknowledge it. Keep going.

Be aware of what you're feeling as that is telling you where you need to put some awareness.

If it feels yucky, dive in, feel it, receive it, clear it, keep going.
If it feels scary, dive in, feel it, receive it, clear it, keep going.
If it feels light, dive in, feel it, receive it, keep going.
If it feels heavy, dive in, feel it, receive it, make a different choice, keep going.

Now is the time to move. Keep going. Keep choosing!

Get clear about what you want to create

It's important to get clear about what you want to create and decide to create it. No matter what. No matter what anyone chooses around you. No matter what other people choose. You have to decide what you want to be and choose to have it. Deciding is key. If you don't decide you become the effect of everyone and everything around you.

First you have to decide to be present in your life and in your day. When I choose being present what I discovered was all the things that took me out of being present. Like my youngest daughter throwing herself on the floor throwing a fit. That put me in anger. I do not desire anger. I do not like to feel angry.

So instead of engaging her when she chose that I said,

"I'm sorry. I can not be present with you when you are choosing to throw a fit. I will be back later." Then I left the room. Instead of spending time, as I used to, being angry, I looked at what was required. Okay, I am aware she maybe hungry, maybe she's tired. Maybe her throwing a fit has nothing to do with me? It's about her and how she is feeling inside. So, what can I do to help make how she is feeling ease? Well, since I don't want to take on her yucky feelings, I can identify that she may need some food. So I make lunch all the while, allowing myself to release, reminding myself I do not desire to feel angry anymore.

When I come back, I do not make her wrong. I do not say, "Let's talk about it" or "Let's talk about why your an awful child."

Nope. I come back into the room and I say, "Hey, are you hungry? Look I made you lunch."

And I sit and I stay present with her. I allow her to eat and I start talking about me. Not her.

And I say,
"You know, I have decided I am only going to engage in stuff that makes me feels good, cause guess what? Feeling bad about myself makes me angry and you know what? I really don't want to be angry anymore. So I'm not going to. I found that hugs make me feel better. Can I have a hug? I know it might seem silly that I need a hug right now, but I kind of do."

And right there, I changed the energy and I created an invitation to something different.

And you know what?

Within two months I changed seven years of emotional outbursts. No more emotional upsets. It's been years since I have had any emotional outbursts from my daughter. Its created an amazing emotional dialog for us to share. She talks candidly about how things make her feel now and it's changed both our lives.

First
I chose what I wanted to be. I chose things for my life that were a mix of both feelings and things.

I choose things like:

I choose ease.
I desired for my life to be easy. I desired for my choices to be easy. Parenting to be easy. Having a body to be easy. My marriage to be easy. I desired for everything I wanted to come to me with ease. I chose ease and I continue to choose ease. I am no longer willing to have struggle or difficulties in my life. If struggle or difficulties arise I know that is a call to action. Right when it appears I am going to call the struggle out, let the struggle know it's not wanted in my life and

release it. I move on with my life. I do not make it significant in any way.

I choose a peaceful existence
I desire to be surrounded by people who have a peaceful existence. I choose people, places and things that feel peaceful. I love situations that cultivate peace in my body and in my being. I am not only choosing to be peaceful, I am demanding those that come into my life choose peace as well. If peace doesn't work for them, that's fine. It's not my choice to make for them. But I do not have to choose to be around people who are in upset. I invite people into my peace. They accept it or deny it. I am unattached to the outcome. See all these choices? These are all choices I am making in my life.

I choose to have lots of money
I choose to have more money than I can spend. I choose for money to always be there for me whenever I require it. I love the support money provides for me and my family. I love being able to choose whatever I desire to choose without making myself wrong. I love to be able to provide for my family. I love the space of ease having money always creates for me.

These are some of my choices. I now invite you to really look at what you would like to choose for you life.

We are going to start first with how you want your life to feel. Bringing your senses into your life creation is a great way to create it faster. As you know your body is a receiving organ so receiving into your body is a great way to actualize.

EXERCISE

Let's first start with "feeling" words. Choose words that expand your energy field. I personally choose words like ease, joy, peace, and expansion. All these words feel amazing to me and I can identify the feelings within them.

I completely understand what ease feels like, but I am not limiting my ease. I am choosing ease, I know what situations and people feel like who are ease to me. I am also aware of how fast I can create ease and receive ease. There are multi-levels of ease I am willing to be and receive. I also can not have a strong point of view about ease or resist things that are hard. If something shows up and it doesn't match the ease I am choosing I release it not resist it.

Let's start by connecting to your breathe. You really want to be present with your body while your choosing energies for your life. Put your barriers down and expand out. Make sure you go all the way out to the space of who you be!

Step one:

What do you desire your life to feel like?
Choose at least three "feelings."
Choose things like ease, joyful, fun, ect.

Then take each one and state:

"Universe I am choosing _____, bring me situations that create _____."
"Universe I have chose _____, bring me _____."
"Universe I am grateful you have brought me _____, Thank you for bringing me _____"
Take a deep breath and receive.
Ask questions about having that space.
Use questions like:

"What can I receive today to have more _____ right away?"
"What can I do or be today to have more _____ right away?" "What can I choose today to receive more _____ right away?"

Remember to ask and receive. You want to become the space of it. You want to get in the habit of asking for these things all day. You can even make it like a game. I am always searching for the ease. Hey, where's the ease? Then when something shows up super easy celebrate it. Like you're a detective searching the world for signs of ease. Every time you "find the ease" you get a prize! Maybe the prize is a smile or a big hug or maybe you get a high five! How fun! Celebrate when you find the energies you desire.

If something shows up or you react in a way that does not match the frequencies you are looking for, that is when you want to remind the universe what you are choosing. Vaporize it and move on. Don't make it significant. Don't throw a pity party. Don't go to all the awful things in your head. Nope. Just release it and move on.

Now let's go to more material things.

I personally have choose the house I desire for now. A car I love to drive. Money in my bank account. The ease of having choices. I love to play with different choices and how the choices create things in my life.

Now you get to choose.

What are some things you would like for your life?

Most important here, you are not trying to figure out how they are going to happen. You are just choosing them. That's key. If you choose having more money than you can spend. You just choose it. You don't try to figure out and conclude how that's going to happen.

You can't say, "well I choose to have more money than I can spend, but I didn't win the lottery, so this doesn't work."

The universe has a million possibilities to deliver you money. But if you decide you can only have that much money if you win the lottery, you just greatly reduced your receiving. But if you choose having more money than you can spend and you don't conclude how that's going to happen, you just choose it and receive the space of it. The universe can provide.

EXERCISE

First start by connecting to your breathe. 1-2-3. 1-2-3. Put your barriers down and expand out. Get into the space of who you be.

Grab a pen and a piece of paper and go!

Write three things you desire to have in your life.
Choose specific things like:
I choose to have more money than I can spend.
I choose to have a car that is fun to drive.
I choose to have a home that feels luxurious.
Notice I am still integrating the senses.

Then state for each one:
"Universe I am choosing _____, bring me situations that create _____."
"Universe I have chose _____, bring me having _____."

"Universe I am grateful you have brought me _____,
Thank you for bringing me _____"
Take a deep breath and receive.

Ask questions daily about having that space.

Use questions like:
"What can I receive today to have more _____ right away?"
"What can I do or be today to have more _____ right away?" "What can I choose today to receive more _____ right away?"

Remember to ask and receive. You want to become the space of it. Just like in the last exercise. Make asking and receiving it a game. The more fun you have the more of it that shows up.

If something shows up or you react in a way that does not match it, that is when you want to remind the universe what you are choosing. Vaporize it and move on.

You are a powerful creator.

You can create anything you choose.

Your choice always creates.

Choose things that feel light and fun and free and soon enough your life will match it!

Stop letting others affect your life

Once I decided what I wanted my life to be like, I got to see how other people's choices affected me. If people choose things that didn't work for me, I was able to stand in my power and tell them. "Look that doesn't actually work for me." Now obviously this was only with things that affected my life on some level.

If their choices didn't have anything to do with me, I was then able to carry on with my own life. I stopped getting emotionally tangled in other people's choices. Because I was clear in my own life. And I understood that I had no control over what other people choose.

If someone is doing something that doesn't work for you, that directly affects your life, you have choices.
- You tell them clearly what doesn't work for you.
- You explain what does work for you.
- Let them know that you will no longer tolerate the behavior that contributes to what does not work for you.
- You stop engaging.
- You revisit the situation later without making the person wrong.
- Let go of what ever happened and allow the behavior to show up differently. This is so important!

This is hard for me to put specifics on because obviously you're going to address a situation with your child differently than you would if it's your parent. The thing to get clear about is, what do you want your life to be like? How do you want to feel? Then actively pursue it releasing and letting go of everything around you that doesn't match it.

Do not make what other people do wrong. Understand that their path is their own. You only have power over what happens in your universe, not someone else's. I find when I address situations and I am clear about what I want to create, the other person realizes what they are creating. It's like you shine a light on a situation. And you give the situation space to change into something different. The reality is that the other person may not have even liked how they were acting or responding. Just like you have gotten caught in actions you didn't like, they may have too.

When you stand in you and speak your truth you will be surprised how fast situations can change. And if they don't pull some energy. And if that doesn't work, be willing to choose you anyway. Even if they want to make you wrong.

This is your universe, you get to decide!

Permission to choose

As you get further into this journey you start to realize that there are lots of places in your life you are not allowed to choose. You start to have the feeling you desire it but this energy comes in and says, "You can't have that" or "You can't choose that." And it literally shuts you down. It turns you off. But today, right now we are changing this. You now have permission to feel, see, hear and have what you would like to choose.

When I first started this journey, I had recently came out of a very traumatic divorce. I had never personally been able to buy myself a new car. My ex-husband had provided me with many, but to consider having one myself, especially in my newly acquired single mom status, it was difficult for me to comprehend.

One of the first things I really started choosing was to have was a new car. There was so much resistance when I even considered it.

"You can't have a new car, you will never afford it."
"How in the world are you going to get a new car?"
" That's never going to happen."

But instead of feeling bad for myself I decided I was going to keep playing with that choice.

Everywhere I went, I would envision myself in a new comfy car.

I would look at the cars on the road and I would say things like, "I will have one of those please."

I was floored at how much resistance I felt to having a majority of the cars I wanted. It was like there was so much energy against my choice. But I kept choosing. Telling myself I will have a new car. I choose it with all my being.

Then a situation arises, not an ideal situation but a situation.

My grandma who was in her 80's at the time, had literally just leased a brand new Malibu. She paid cash for the entire three year lease. Her memory was failing along with her health and she had to be put into a nursing home just months after purchasing it. And although it was unfortunate the universe heard my request! My mom told me that since my grandma was no longer driving my grandma said I could have her car for the remainder of the lease!

It was the first time in my life I had done such a big ask and voilà!

Without figuring it out, without trying to make it work, without making it right or wrong, a brand new vehicle showed up in my life that was already paid for, for the next two and a half years!

It was a pivotal time for me. I really felt how my choice created that. My grandmother and I were very close. We talked about the car and she was so happy I was able to drive it and that it worked great for me. It felt like she was doing her part in helping me to create a new reality. It really solidified for me that I can have everything I want to choose and it doesn't have to be hard.

The universe does have my back.

Get out of conclusion and choose what you want

Staying out of conclusion is key to expanding yourself and your life.

You cannot successfully create a life that expands you by continually looping in conclusion and figuring out.

You must integrate a series of choices based on how they feel. You will not build a life that creates ease by planning every second and then worrying about if it will go as planned.

You live a life that works and has ease by living in the moment, by staying present in every second.

Asking and receiving for exactly what you desire.
Be open to possibilities.

Stop projecting and expecting.

Take responsibility for your actions.

And choose your life.

No one else is going to create a life for you that works for you. This is your Universe. You get to decide.

Don't make money wrong

Let's face it. Having money definitely makes life easier. Having money creates more choices. And having money opens up new possibilities.

So why do we make money so wrong? Money is not bad or wrong. It is not the root of all evil. And it's definitely not something you should ever make wrong.

Money is a tool that you use to create a better life. There is no shortage of money in this world. In fact, less than five percent of the world holds over ninety percent of the wealth. You know why? Because they have convinced us all that having money, enjoying money and desiring money is wrong. Can you perceive all that wrongness that comes up even reading this?

It's like you are not allowed to like money, have money or enjoy money. Do you want to spend the rest of your existence here struggling to have money?Or would you care to just start asking and choosing to have ease with money and have money?

That energy you have coming up is resistance to money, that is the very energy that keeps you from having it. The universe is a very abundant place. There are literally billions of dollars of unaccounted for money.

Why can't you have more?

Why do you have to resist money and make it wrong?

Why can't you just receive more?

There's enough for all of us to have enough.

Every single one of us can have money without anyone having lack. You can't have it because you have been programmed to resist it. Every one of our generations has been taught to make money wrong.

What if you could ask for money and it didn't mean anything about you? What if money was ok to have and receive? What if you could choose to have money now? Wouldn't that contribute so much more to your life?

You being locked up and limited isn't contributing to this planet. You making a conscious choice right now to have money, to create wealth, and to go beyond lack creates a cycle of more for everyone. Just think of everything you would be able to create and contribute too when you have a continuous flow of wealth.

As an empath, I know personally when I have more money I contribute to everyone around me, just like you will. Possibly you dream about winning the lottery and paying off your family members' homes? Or maybe you have a desire to own a healing center where you help people heal from depression and disorders?

As empathic people, much of what we want is centered around helping others. If you could have millions of dollars, how would you contribute to this planet?

What if you could have the money now?

I am choosing to have a more money than I can spend, universe bring me more money than I can spend.

Getting out of money upset

Money is just energy. It's not vital to existence. You can exist with or without money. Sure having money definitely allows for your life to be easier and potentially better on some level but you have to separate the want and need of money from the desire to have it.

Money listens to the energy you give it.

If you stay in constant worry and upset over money, money will always give you something to worry and be upset about.
Clear the way you feel about money just as we have been clearing the way you feel about everything else. Give yourself space for the money. Celebrate the space of money.

If money was your friend and you called money up and said, "Hey money! Want to come over to my house? I'm going to sit around and be mad at you. I'm going to worry incessantly about you. I am going to tell you over and over how I'm scared I won't have enough of you and I am going to obsess every minute I'm with you."

Would you come over and hang out with me? Of course not!

You are not going to hang out with anyone who repeatedly makes you wrong, worries about you and/or obsesses over you. And neither is money!

Money is light and free and fun.

If you want to have money, you too must be light and free and fun with money. Or it's never coming to your party.

Conscious clearings for money to show up for you

When I first started my conscious journey and I became aware of how much my limiting points of views were creating for me, one of the experiments I played with was, what was everything I would not do for money?

What was everything I had decided was wrong way to get money?

My list went something like this:
- I wouldn't rob a bank.
- I wouldn't be a stripper or a prostitute.
- I wouldn't steal from someone or from a business.
- I wouldn't sell my body for money.

Honestly, I know my list was long but I have no idea what else was on there!

     The thing about the "things" you have decided are bad, once you decide that about them you can never receive from someone who would choose them.

     So if you would never be a stripper, you can never receive from anyone who would be a stripper or who has been in the past. Now we aren't just talking money, we're talking just in general. You can't receive information, energy, attention, any of it. What ends up happening to us is our stored viewpoints of right and wrong start shutting us down from the world. They start creating separation from us and everyone else. And although we aren't sure why we feel so separate, the reality is, it's all energy. The thing is when you clear these places out, you do not actually have to choose any of them. Like when I was talking about robbing a bank. Obviously, I am not planning to rob a bank anytime soon. But if I hold onto the viewpoint robbing a bank is terrible, awful, and the worst choice ever, then I can never receive from someone capable of doing it. And let's really look at that for a moment. This is all lifetimes!

If you have a resistance to something, you have more than likely been and done that. So if you have a ton of resistance, tons of points of views about it you probably know a lot about it, meaning you potentially did it at some point in your life. Therefore, you are cutting yourself off from parts and pieces of you! When you clear the resistance and the points of views, you are releasing yourself.

Also just because I don't have tons of resistance to robbing a bank doesn't mean I have to choose it or ever will choose it. It just means I don't have to make it wrong. I can see it's just a choice. And as long as there are people resisting the choice of it, it upholds the space for it to exist. If I release my resistance to it and become neutral. I am no longer creating it as a possibility. Therefore I am changing the world by changing my charge to it.

I spent some time and space one day really getting clear about all the things I had points of views about, people, places, and professions. And you know what happened just a short time after?

I owned a healing center at this time. I did massage, reiki, tons of energy healing stuff and readings. We had a psychic fair one weekend and these two women came in desperate for help. One woman told me her friend, who I recognized right away, needed my help. And I knew instantly what was going on.

The "friend" was someone I knew well. She had no idea who I was but I knew her and in fact, I personally had judged this woman in the past. She was a teacher in the local elementary. Her classroom was across the hall from my daughters classroom.

She came to school daily scantily dressed in her high heels and her short tight dresses. Man did us moms talk about this women. The rumor around the school was she was an exotic dancer by night. Every day after school, she was out of the building before us, as I picked my child up daily. Out she rushed to her car as I had heard she had another job to make it to.

When I saw her before me, I instantly knew. I literally had just spent hours clearing out my viewpoints around people who choose to work in the sex industry and right here before my very eyes stood a woman I knew who worked for it.

As I took her into my therapy room I could literally feel the projections of wrongness covering her body. The way she processed information was over processed and her body was the effect of all that judgment. She told me that day how she just wanted to die, how she had already tried many times before. She needed some help.

She was pivotal to my consciousness journey. She taught me so much about thoughts, feelings, and emotions. She also helped me see how easy I could guide someone through judgment. She came to see me for many months as we peeled away these layers. And you know what I discovered? She made the choice to be a dancer because she liked it. She liked the way she felt and she loved the attention she got from it. It really changed my world.

And I know that if I hadn't done what I had done prior there is no way this woman would have come and seen me. I helped her just as much as she helped me. I get now why I would never want to resist anyone. She was a beautiful soul who taught me a ton about myself and my capacities.

Let's peel away those layers for you. In the next exercise let's get clear about everything you would never do for money.

EXERCISE

Grab a pen and a pad of paper.

Make a list of everything you would never do for money. Think of everything, get real creative Maybe you would never milk a cow? Or Maybe you would never serve food or cook food in a restaurant?

Once the list is complete look at each thing.

First you want to clear out everywhere you decided it was bad or wrong.

"Where is everywhere I have decided, ex. robbing a bank was bad or wrong? Vaporize.

Then clear the polarity on it.
Where is everywhere I
Aligned and agreed - to robbing a bank
Resisted and reacted - to robbing a bank
Defended for - robbing a bank
Defended against - robbing a bank
Righteous for - robbing a bank
Righteous against - robbing a bank

Do these for each and every thing on your list. Do this with the intention you are clearing your resistance to it, not because you are going to choose it. Just because you release yourself from the polarity of it doesn't mean you're going to choose it!
Give yourself some gratitude! You have come so far! Your willingness to clear yourself out from underneath all these viewpoints is helping the world heal. I am so grateful for you and your choice to keep moving!

Allowing the universe to gift you

As you continue on in your consciousness journey, your life will change dramatically. When you function in asking and receiving, being space, staying expanded and asking questions, you can expect that the universe is going to start gifting you. When that starts to happen you cannot make it wrong!

You can expect to receive things for free, free food, free gifts, massive discounts, and so on. You cannot make that wrong! You equally cannot resist it. If you resist the gift you're completely counteracting all this work you are doing.

You are a receiver. This reality has taught you receiving is wrong. That was a lie. That is why you have felt so locked up and so limited. You are here to receive things. Receive.

Do not refuse gifts and do not make a gift wrong!

We are in a very powerful time of awakening currently. We are all releasing and paying back karmic debts. If someone wants to give you something for free, let them! Receive it. Don't resist it. Allow the universe to gift you greater than ever before.

Be the space of ease you wish to see in this world!

Receive everyone and everything!

You are an infinite being with infinite choice and possibilities. You are here on this amazing adventure to be a contribution to this planet and the people. If you could only see the gift you are to this world, the resources you have at your disposal, the infinite amount of things waiting to contribute. You would see that nothing is outside of your possibility. You really can have everything you desire to have. You can be anything you would like to be. All it takes is the choice and the ability to receive.

Now it's your turn to take all these tools you learned and embrace that you are the creator of your reality. Now is the time to create something grand. No more making yourself wrong. No more playing small. You are limitless. Time to shine!

I am grateful for you and your choice to read my book. I thank you for your contribution to consciousness. And if you take anything away from this book, please know that it's your universe and you get to decide. You are a powerful creator.

Much love to you. If you love this book please share the love with your friends! Isn't it time we all become magical creators of our own realities?

If you are interested in further information about what I offer and or further training check out the next section for details on how to step more into who you be!

What to choose now?

If you want more from me you are in luck! I have an abundance of audio programs to expand you even further! What are you looking for?

First things first! There is a free series waiting for you with lots of fun consciousness stuff!
You can check it out at www.jamie-bates.com which you will also find all of the additional programs.

Need some emotional clearing? Check out my programs playing in polarity and creating consciousness.

Want to learn how to receive more? Check these out!
Learn to master the ask and receive with:
30 days of Ask and Receive.
Expand your money flows with:
Magic Money Boot Camp or
30 days of Money Pulls
Be more magic:
30 days of Magic and Miracles
Have more love:
30 days of love
Want more peace and ease:
30 days of surrender
Want to build your business energetically:
30 days of business creation
Want to reset your life:
Reset and Relaunch
Want to receive from everyone and everything:
Ask and Receive

Additionally I offer group coaching and private coaching for those ready to dive in and go beyond the stuff sticking them.

I also have a ton of free stuff from my podcast Expand Your Reality to soundcloud and YouTube.

You can find my radio show on iTunes, YouTube and Podbean and at www.expandyourreality.net

If your ready to take your life to the next level join me and let's expand your reality now!

About the Author

Jamie Bates is a mother, wife, world wide consciousness facilitator and intuitive guide. Jamie lives in Michigan with her husband, her youngest two daughters, 2 dogs, 2 cats and her green cheek conure. Jamie enjoys visiting her oldest daughter in Chicago, traveling, spending time with her family and of course helping people release limitations.

Jamie began her journey in her teens when she started diving one on one with a local angel healer to expand her gifts and capacities as an intuitive. Jamie always knew she was different. She knew things about people no one else knew or was acknowledging.

Jamie started helping people with readings, guidance and healing in her twenties. She became a Reiki master and healing touch practitioner. She found it was very easy for her to pinpoint the source point for people's emotional and physical pains. She found she could not only identify the upsets in their life, she could also help them completely untangle and release them. She threw herself into discovering the secrets to releasing karmic baggage and untangling people from lifetimes of deep inner pain. She went to massage school and discovered she had a natural ability to release pain that had been plaguing people for decades and she could place her hands on someone's body and go to the memory that created that pain even if it was lifetimes ago.

Jamie has helped countless numbers of people release diseases, disorders, emotional traumas, and physical ailments. For over two decades she has worked countless hours learning and developing tools and processes that help people expand beyond limitations and stand in their knowing. Jamie has perfected the energetic synthesis of being a frequency healer, where just by listening and or reading the pages of her book your body and being will change and heal.

Jamie also has used these very tools to heal her own children after a traumatic divorce, empower them to stand in their own truth and to create massive shifts in her home life. For more information about Jamie or her journey please visit her online at www.jamie-bates.com

This book is a combination of decades of personal study, growth, and information I have collected while working one on one with clients.

Jamie currently works from home creating life changing programs, audios, podcasts and personal sessions that help people around the world create massive waves of change in their lives.

Some tools listed in this book come from the following sources:
Access Consciousness: www.accessconsciousness.com
Jaden Fox: www.jaden-fox.com

Made in the USA
Middletown, DE
07 April 2019